Creators'
Self-Promotion:
In-House Graphics

クリエイターの
自社ツール＆ワークスペース

Contents

自社ツールとワークスペースから見えてくる、理念とこだわり

どのような事務所にしたいのか、
その想いは事務所名にはもちろんのこと、ロゴや名刺をはじめとする自社ツールや
ワークスペースにも表れるものだと思います。
そんな名刺や封筒等の自社ツールは、初対面の人に対して、
いわば自己紹介のような役割を果たしているといっても過言ではありません。
事務所が大切にしていること、強く抱いている想い、
それらをを示す重要なコミュニケーションツールのひとつなのです。

例えば"あたたかさ"を重視して、あえてロゴに手書き文字を採用している事務所もあれば、人との関わりを
大切にしたいという想いから、名刺交換の場でコミュニケーションが生まれるようにと、名刺にちょっと
した仕掛けを施しているところもあります。また、できる限り要素を削ぎおとし、名刺・封筒ともに
普遍的なデザインを追求している事務所も。
大切にしている想いの表現方法は、事務所の数だけ多種多様に存在するものだと思います。

本書では、国内外のデザイン事務所や広告代理店をはじめ、写真事務所・スタイリス
ト・イラストレーター・建築事務所など、様々なジャンルのクリエイターが使用する、
デザイン性に優れた自社ツールとワークスペースを特集します。
クリエイティブな仕事が生まれるワークスペースも興味深く、
テーブルや棚、照明にいたるまで、その空間にはクリエイターの
世界観が凝縮されています。

新しく事務所を立ち上げるときはもちろん、他社のステーショ
ナリーのデザインを手掛ける際、また、ステーショナリー
以外のグラフィックツールを制作する際の刺激となる
アイデアソースとして活用いただけたなら幸いです。

最後になりましたが、お忙しい中、
長期にわたり快くご協力ください
ました出品者の皆様に、この場
をお借りして心より御礼申
し上げます。

Ideas and attention to detail gleaned from a company's self-promotional business tools and workspaces

What kind of company do I want to create?
The answer to that question can be seen in the choice of company name, and also in the look of the company's logo, business cards and other self-promotional tools, as well as its workspaces.

To say that a company's self-promotional business tools such as business cards and envelopes serve as a form of self-introduction to first-time clients is by no means an overstatement. These tools are an important means of communication, showing outsiders what a company's values are and what a company feels strongly about.

For example, a company that wants to emphasize "warmth" may use hand-written characters in its logo, or one that values the human interface may use some device or other on its business cards to stimulate communication when business cards are exchanged. A company may also decide to strip away many of the possible design elements to achieve a universal design. There as many diverse ways of expressing the ideas that a company holds dear as there are companies themselves.

This book features the stationery and workspaces, selected for their outstanding design quality, belonging to design offices and advertising agencies both in and outside Japan, as well as creatives working across a variety of design-related genres including photographers, stylists, illustrators and architects.

The workspaces where all this creative endeavour takes place are also of interest, and it is within these spaces that we can see in a condensed form the designer's way of looking at the world around them, from his or her choice of table or desk to the lighting.

We hope that this book proves to be a source of exciting ideas for those of you who are designing your own company stationery for the first time or for another company, or creating some other graphic design-based business tools.

In closing, we wish to express our heartfelt thanks to all the contributors who took time out of their busy lives to participate in the production of this book.

Editorial Note

(A) 事務所名
Office name

(B) 業種
Type of business and industry

(C) ロゴ・ツールのデザインコンセプト
Concept of logo and tools

(D) 制作国
Country from which the works have been submitted

(E) 制作スタッフ
Creative staff

PL: プランナー Planner
PR: プロデューサー Producer
CD: クリエイティブ・ディレクター Creative Director
AD: アート・ディレクター Art Director
D: デザイナー Designer
P: フォトグラファー Photographer
I: イラストレーター Illustrator
DF: デザイン会社 Design Firm
SB: 作品提供者 Submittor

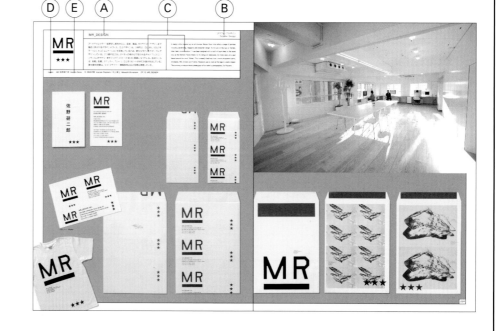

※ 上記以外の制作者呼称は省略せずに掲載しています。
All other production titles are unabbreviated.

※ スタッフクレジットと作品につくアルファベットは、制作者を示す照合番号です。
The alphabet indicated after the works and the creative staff name, it is
the reference number to show the person who is in charge of the work.

※ 作品提供者の意向によりデータの一部を記載していない場合があります。
Please note that some credit information has been omitted at the request of the submittor.

※ 各企業名に付随する、"株式会社、（株）"および"有限会社、（有）"は表記を省略させていただきました。
The " kabushiki gaisha (K.K.) " and " yugen gaisha " (Ltd.) portions of all names have been omitted.

※ 本書に記載された企業名・商品名は、掲載各社の商標または登録商標です。
The company and product names that appear in this book are published and / or registered trademarks.

掲載作品について　About the works

• 名刺は約60%のサイズで掲載しています。その他のツールについては、それぞれほぼ比率を合わせて掲載しています。
The size of the business cards appearing in this book are reduced to 60% of the original while the size of other graphics depends.
However, the comparative size of multiple graphics of one creator is kept the same as the original.

• 名刺や封筒に記載されている住所や電話番号、メールアドレスなどの個人情報の中で、非公開のものについては画像処理を施し、
架空の情報となっています。
The personal information in the graphics has been changed to dummy information
unless those are public or prior approvals have been received.

Creators' Self-Promotion: In-House Graphics

©2008 PIE BOOKS

PIE BOOKS
2-32-4, Minami-Otsuka, Toshima-ku, Tokyo 170-0005 Japan
Phone: +81-3-5395-4811   Fax: +81-3-5395-4812
E-mail: editor@piebooks.com   sales@piebooks.com
http://www.piebooks.com/

ISBN978-4-89444-699-1 C3070   Printed in Japan

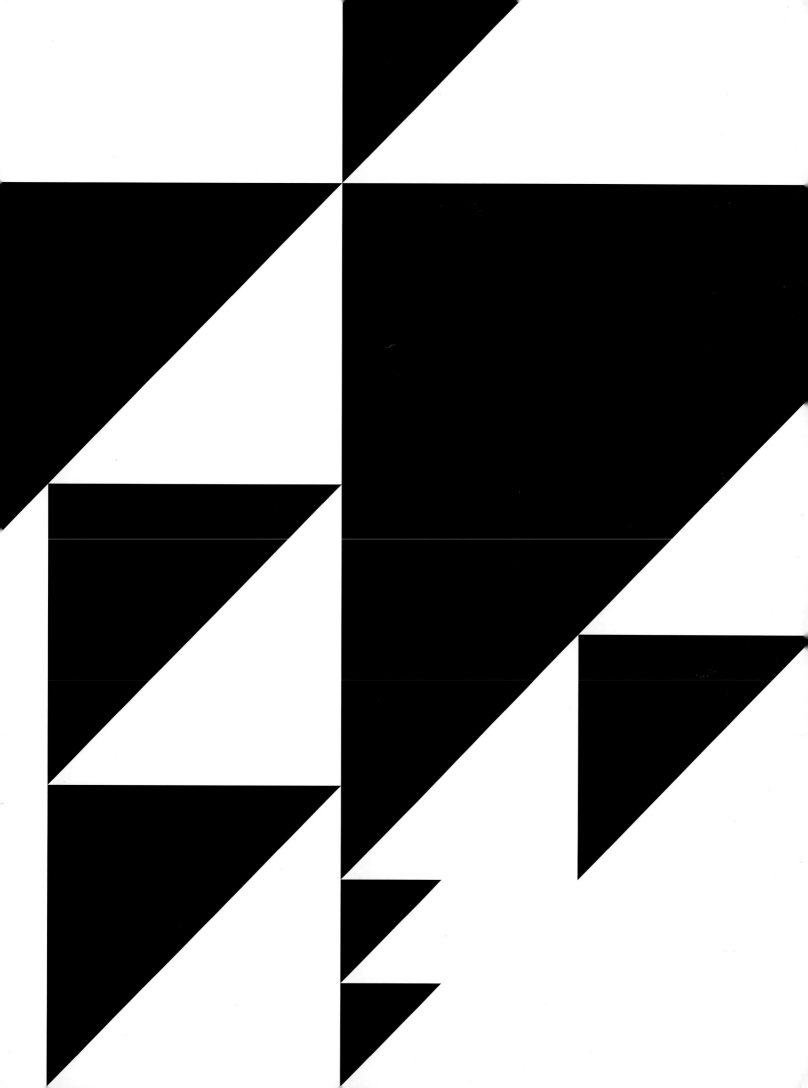

MR_DESIGN

アートディレクター・佐野研二郎を中心に、広告、雑誌、キャラクターデザインまで幅広く手がけるデザインオフィス。ロゴデザインは、SIMPLE、CLEAR、BOLDをテーマとしたコミュニケーションを目指しているため、骨太なラインをモチーフにデザインしている。三つ星のロゴはレストランの格付けで知られるガイドブック「ミシュラン」にあやかり、★が3つで「ミスター」と掛けた洒落になっている。自社ツールは、名刺、封筒、ステッカー、Tシャツ。ロゴをリピートさせて力強さを出している。夏仕様の封筒は、フォトグラファー・間部百合の氷の写真を使用している。

A design office headed up by art director, Kenjiro Sano, that offers a range of services including advertising, magazine and character design. As the aim of the logo is "simple, clear, bold communication," it has been designed with a motif of heavy lines. In the same way as the Michelin Guide known for its ratings of restaurants, the three stars are a pun based around the word "Mister." The company's business tools consist of business cards, envelopes, DM, stickers and T-shirts. Repeated use is made of the logo to create impact. The summery envelopes have a photograph of ice taken by photographer, Yuri Manabe.

Japan　AD: 佐野研二郎 Kenjiro Sano　D: 岡本和樹 Kazuki Okamoto / 村上雅士 Masashi Murakami　DF, S: MR_DESIGN

ステッカー Sticker

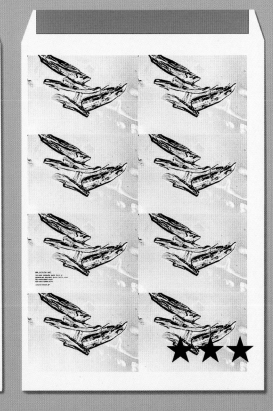

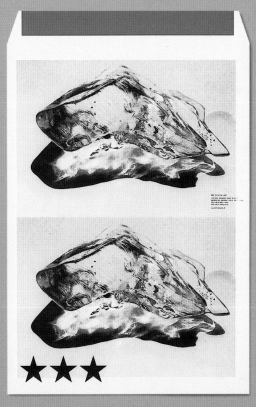

POOL Inc.

広告制作会社
Advertising Production Company

博報堂から独立したクリエイティブディレクター・小西利行が2006年に設立した広告制作会社。社名の由来は、人が集まって、楽しんで、気持ちよく回遊していく場所でありたいという想いからネーミングされた。オフィスも白を基調に、プールのキラキラした気持ちよさを表現した透明のアクリルを使用している。ロゴデザインは社名の通りプールをシンボル化したもの。自社ツールは、名刺、封筒、原稿用紙、紙袋など。名刺の表面には、男性スタッフは男性、女性スタッフには女性のピクトグラムをそれぞれ使用している。

An advertising production company established in 2006 by creative director Toshiyuki Konishi. The company name contains the idea of a place where people get together, have fun and relax. As Pool's offices are also in a basic tone of white, a transparent acrylic that expresses the glittering water in a swimming pool was used. The design for the logo contains as one might expect, a symbol of a swimming pool. The company's tools include business cards, envelopes, a manuscript paper and paper bags. On the front of the business card, male staff members have a pictogram for a man, and on the women's cards, that of a woman.

Japan   CD: 小西利行 Toshiyuki Konishi   AD: 後 智仁 Tomohito Ushiro   D: 鈴木 海 Kai Suzuki   CW: 小林麻衣子 Maiko Kobayashi   DF: スーデ Sude   Architect: 林 順孝 Yoritaka Hayashi   S: POOL Inc.

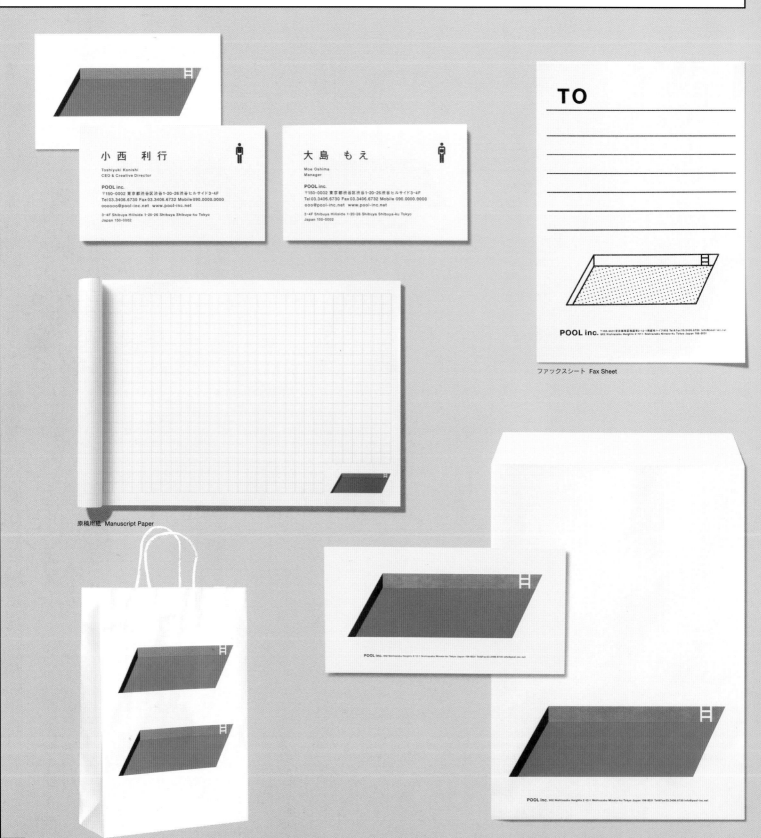

ファックスシート Fax Sheet

原稿用紙 Manuscript Paper

クリスマスカード
Christmas Card

We Wish You A Happy New Year.

POOL inc. 小西 利行／小林 麻衣子／大島 もえ 〒106-0031 東京都港区西麻布2-12-1 西麻布ハイツ902 Tel 03.3406.8730 www.pool-inc.net

博報堂ケトル　HAKUHODO Kettle Inc.

博報堂と東北新社が2006年に設立したクリエイティブエージェンシー。「アイデアで世の中を沸騰させたい」との想いから、社名に「やかん」を意味する「ケトル」という言葉を付けた。ロゴデザインは、gooddesigncompanyのアートディレクター・水野 学が担当。ロゴは、数あるやかんのデザインから最もシンプルなものを追求した。自社ツールは名刺、会社案内、台割用ノート、年賀状、トートバッグ、Tシャツ。ポップな「やかん」が効果を発揮しやすいツールを様々なアートディレクターと開発している。

A creative agency established in 2006 by Hakuhodo Co. Ltd. and the Tohokushinsha Film Corporation. The company was named "kettle" from the idea of "simmering ideas and exciting the world." Art director, Manabu Mizuno, of the gooddesigncompany was responsible for the design of the logo and the company's business tools. The aim of the logo was an image of a plain and simple kettle." The company's business tools are business cards, a company profile, notebooks, New Year cards, a tote bag and T-shirts. Development has centred on the pop "kettle," the effect of which is easy to demonstrate.

Japan　CD: 嶋 浩一郎　Koichiro Shima / 木村健太郎　Kentaro Kimura / 船木 研　Ken Funaki　　AD: 水野 学　Manabu Mizuno (Logo & a) / 浜辺明弘　Akihiro Hamabe (b) / タイムトロン　Timetron (c) /
中村圭介　Keisuke Nakamura (d) / 舞木和哉　Kazuya Mougi (e) / GEOGRAPH (Office Design)　　PL: 橋田和明　Kazuaki Hashida　　PR: 森川 俊　Toshi Morikawa

a

d ノート　Notebook

a 封筒　Envelope

a Tシャツ　T-Shirt

c トートバッグ　Tote Bag

a 紙袋　Paper Bag

Boil the World, Kettle

c 社章
Company Emblem

b 年賀状 (2007年) New Year Card

b DM

b 年賀状 (2008年) New Year Card

やかんは赤坂へ

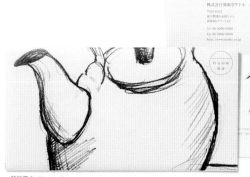

e 移転案内 Moving Announcement

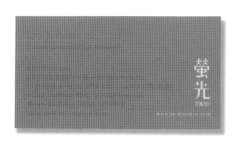

螢光TOKYO　KEI-KO TOKYO

クリエイティブエージェンシー
Creative Agency

元博報堂のアートディレクター・手島 領とCMプランナー前田康二によって2005年に設立された、ユニークで心に届く表現をつくるクリエイティブ・ユニット。広告制作を中心に、全てのクリエイティブ領域で活躍している。ロゴは手島 領がデザインし、自社ツールは、2006年に設立されたデザインオフィス「DESIGN BOY Inc.」が作成した。ロゴには漢字の強さ、昭和レトロ、2人ユニット、といった要素が盛り込まれている。自社ツールは名刺、封筒、紙袋、会社案内、クリアファイル。名刺を両面PP加工するなど、全体的に「ポップでひと癖ある」デザインを意識している。

A creative unit established in 2005 by Ryo Teshima (former art director at Hakuhodo) and commercial planner, Koji Maeda. It concentrates mainly on advertising but is also involved in the entire range of creative domains. The DESIGN BOY Inc designed the company's business tools. The logo shows an awareness of the strength of kanji characters, a nostalgia for the Showa years and the idea that two people form a unit. The company's business tools consist of business cards, envelopes, paper bags, a company profile and clear files. Both sides of the business cards have undergone a polypropylene process and the general design shows a consciousness of a "quirky, pop design."

Japan　CD: 螢光TOKYO　KEI-KO TOKYO　AD, D, DF, S: DESIGN BOY

クリアファイル Clear File

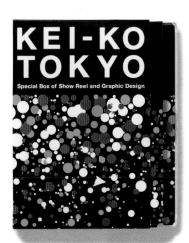

DVD

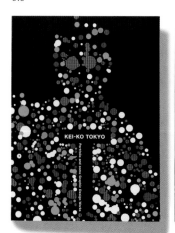

10　Ten

柿木原政広が2007年に設立し、広告、CI、ブランディングなど幅広い分野で活動するデザイン事務所。シンプルにどれだけのことを伝えられるかを考え、印象的なネーミングにしたい、という想いから数字の「10」と名付けた。そこには、ミクロの「点」とマクロの「天」という両方の意味が込められている。ロゴは、以前制作したカレンダーの「10月」に使用したてんとう虫のモチーフをもとにデザイン。自社ツールは、名刺、封筒、会社設立時の挨拶状。封筒は、開封部分が波状になっており、シンプルながらも遊び心を感じさせるデザインとなっている。

A design office established in 2007 by Masahiro Kakinokihara who is active in a wide range of fields including advertising, CI and branding. The striking company name 10 was chosen after considering the amount of information that is capable of being conveyed in a simple way. The word "ten" is a play on two Japanese words: "ten" meaning "dot" (micro) and "ten" meaning "heaven" (macro). The design of the logo is based on a motif of a ladybug. The seal part of the envelopes is in the shape of wave, a design effect that, although simple, incorporates a sense of fun.

Japan　　AD, D: 柿木原政広 Masahiro Kakinokihara　　DF, S: 10　Ten

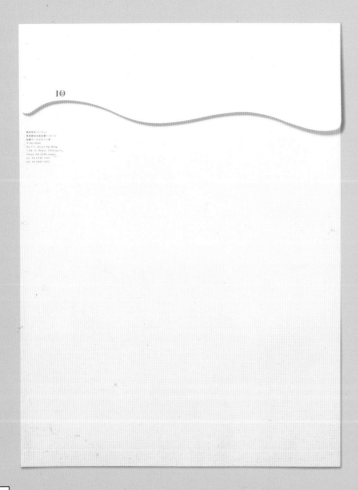

設立案内 Establishment Invitation

GRAPH

グラフ　GRAPH

GRAPH（昭和8年／1933年創業）はデザインとファクトリー（印刷工場）のセクションをもつ本社を兵庫県に構え、東京にデザインセクションをおいている。GRAPHでは、ビジュアルコミュニケーションをトータルにつくりあげ、保守管理を行っている。パースがついたように見えるロゴは、受け取る側の経験や心理状態によって見え方が変わるというデザインの本質にフォーカスしてつくられており、また、名刺などのツールは「色は光によって認識される」というコンセプトに基づき、そのコンセプトに合致した「グラフイエロー」と呼ばれる自社開発の蛍光色インキを使用している。

デザイン / 印刷 / 知的財産管理
Design / Printing / Intellectual property management

A design and printing company. Principal designer is Issay Kitagawa. The head office and factory are in Hyogo Prefecture and the main design section is in Tokyo. GRAPH provides a complete range of services regarding visual communication, including graphic design, branding and printing. The size of each letter in the GRAPH logo can either be interpreted as becoming larger or smaller, depending on the experiences and psychological state of the viewer. The fluorescent GRAPH yellow ink is based on the concept that, "color is acknowledged by light".

Japan　CD, AD: 北川一成　Issay Kitagawa　DF, S: グラフ　GRAPH

納品書　Delivery Slip

領収書　Receipt

ファックスシート　Fax Sheet

ステッカー
Sticker

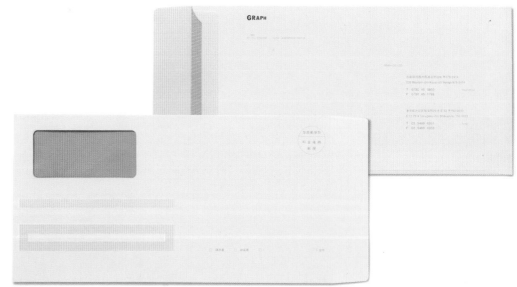

封筒　Envelope

ステッカー Sticker

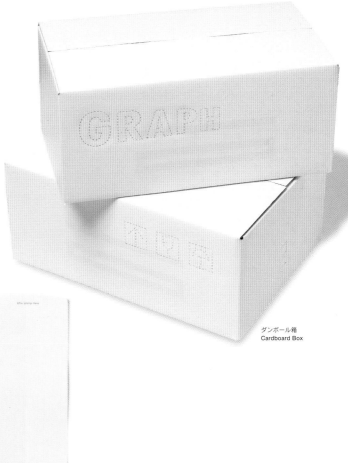

ダンボール箱
Cardboard Box

封筒 Envelope

会社案内 Company Brochure

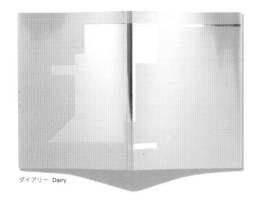

ダイアリー Dairy

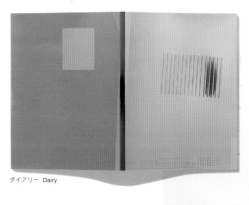

ダイアリー Dairy

8 2008 GRAPH

sun	mon	tue	wed	thu	fri	sat
					1	2
3	4	5	6	7	8	9
10	11	12	13	14	15	16
17	18	19	20	21	22	23
24	25	26	27	28	29	30
31						

カレンダー Calendar

ホーム　home inc.

広告、デザインのみにとどまらず、あらゆる分野をトータルでディレクションするデザイン事務所。ホームベースや将棋の駒のようにも見えるロゴのコンセプトは、homeの頭文字である「h」と「家」をかたどったもの。自社ツールのアートディレクションは、1999年に工藤ワビ良平と中西サビー志によって結成されたデザインユニット「ワビサビ」が制作。ツールの種類は名刺、封筒、年賀状。封筒は、繰り返し使用しても味わいが出る質感を狙った。年賀状は、シンプルながら印象深いものに仕上がるよう配慮し、型抜き等の特殊加工を施している。

A design office that doesn't stop at just advertising and design but is involved in a multitude of fields. The logo resembles a house looks simultaneously like the letter H in "home." The artwork for the company's own business tools was produced by wabisabi, a design unit formed in 1999 by Ryohei "Wabi" Kudo and Kazushi "Sabi" Nakanishi. The business tools include business cards, envelopes and New Year cards. The aim for the envelopes was for them to look good even if they were used several times. The New Year cards, although simple, were created to make an impact and underwent a special die-cutting process.

Japan　　AD, D: ワビサビ　wabisabi　　DF, S: ホーム　home inc.

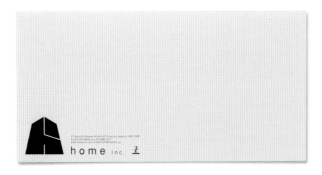

年賀状　New Year Card

シンガタ　Shingata Inc.

佐々木 宏と黒須美彦を中心に2003年に設立されたクリエイティブエージェンシー。「広告を元気にしたい」＝「企業自体や広告を見る人を元気にしたい」という想いが会社のコンセプト。ロゴデザインは、アートディレクター・仲條正義氏が手がけ、直角をベースとしたデザインに。封筒などの各ツールにも、ロゴと同様のマス目が活かされている。事務所内装のコンセプトは、ドラエもんに出てくる「空き地」。カーブした壁は土管を、水道は学校の蛇口を、収納の役割も果たす跳び箱や砂場など、遊び心が溢れたワークスペースとなっている。

A creative agency established in 2003. The company's concept is "cheerful advertising makes for cheerful companies and cheerful potential customers." The logo, which is based on right angles, was designed by art director Masayoshi Nakajo. The same square shape as the logo has been used on all the tools including the envelopes. The concept for the interior design of its offices is based on the "empty lot" that appears in the Doraemon cartoons. A fun workspace has been created using drainpipes as curved walls, faucets from elementary schools, and with vaulting horses and sandboxes used for storage.

Japan　AD: 福田高行 Takayuki Soeda (a) / 水口克夫 Katsuo Mizuguchi / 水野 学 Manabu Mizuno　D: gooddesigncompany / 貝塚智子 Tomoko Kaizuka (a)　DF, S: シンガタ　Shingata Inc.

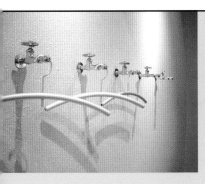
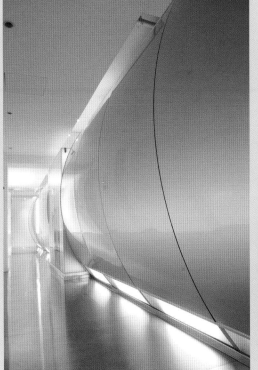

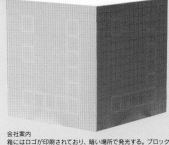

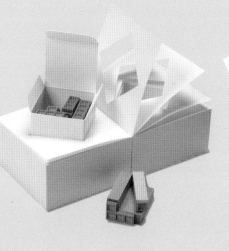

会社案内
箱にはロゴが印刷されており、暗い場所で発光する。ブロックメモの中の箱にはスタンプが入っていて、組み合わせると「シンガタ」の文字ができあがる仕組みになっている。
Company Brochure
The logo is printed on the box, and glows in the dark. The box inside the notepad block contains stamps designed to form the characters "shingata" when combined.

こんにちは。

この暑いのに、なんですが、「シンガタ」が、スタートしました。

どう思います？「シンガタ」という名前。妻向きは、広告のシンガタをつくる乞。

と息巻いておりますが、どうなんでしょう？ はたして。

さて、この企てにノッてしまった6人プラス1が、これまで応援してくださった方々、

これから応援していただきたい方々を、「シンガタ・オフィス」に、ご招待させていただきます。

たいしたおもてなしはできませんが、シャンパン、ワイン、ビール、ショーチューあります。

ちょっと、顔だしていただければ、うれしく思います。

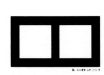

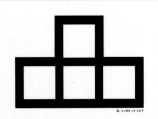

設立案内　マス目はステッカーになっており、オープニング・パーティの来場者にメッセージを書き込んでもらい、事務所の壁に貼れるようにした。
Establishment Invitation　The blocks are stickers, so that guests at the opening party could write messages for sticking on the office walls.

023

	デザインサービス design service co., ltd.	グラフィックデザイン Graphic Design
design service	アートディレクター・池田亨史、高尾元樹、井上由美子、藤城敦子を中心に、3S（simple、smile、surprise）をコンセプトにしているデザイン事務所。自社ツールは名刺、封筒、レターヘッド、DM、年賀状、マンガノート。封筒、名刺に使用している用紙は、コート紙にロウ引き加工を施して半透明にしているため、中に入っている絵柄入りの紙（3種あり）が透けて見える仕組みとなっている。また、名刺も異なった絵柄のものを3種類制作している。（http://designservice.jp）	A design office headed up by art director Takafumi Ikeda, Motoki Takao, Yumiko Inoue, Atsuko Fujishiro that is based on the concept of 3S (simple, smile, surprise). The company's business tools consist of business cards, envelopes, letterhead, DM, New Year cards, manga notebooks and a company profile. The paper selected for the envelopes and the business cards was coated and underwent a waxing process to make it translucent. The paper with illustrations (three variations) on the inside is therefore visible from the outside. The business cards have also been produced in three different designs.

Japan   AD: 池田亨史 Takafumi Ikeda   D: 高尾元樹 Motoki Takao   I: 鈴木規子 Noriko Suzuki   DF, S: デザインサービス design service co., ltd.

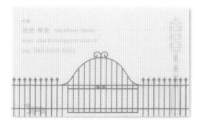
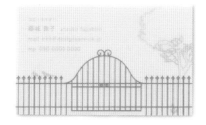

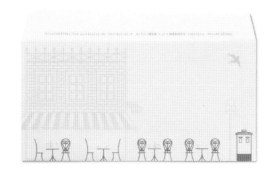

ノート Notebook

EMMI

ロンドンに所在するグラフィックデザインスタジオEMMI。名刺はメモノートを用いたデザイン。自社プロモーション用に作られたバッジはイギリスとフィンランドで販売している。環境のために封筒を再利用しており、梱包用テープに便箋のカラーストライプやリサイクルロゴのグラフィックを取り入れてリサイクル便箋であることを主張している。

グラフィックデザイン
Graphic Design

EMMI is a graphic design studio based in London. Business card is based on a stationery idea. Badges used as a self-promotional tool is sold at shops in the UK and Finland. The studio uses recycled envelopes and the tape used to seal them shows graphic shapes hinting envelopes, postal stripes and arrows for recycling.

UK   D: Emmi Salonen   DF, S: EMMI

EMMI SALONEN
Graphic Designer
hello@emmi.co.uk
www.emmi.co.uk
077 5200 1311

バッジ Badge

ロクディ　6D

グラフィックデザイナー・木住野彰悟と空間デザイナー・大坪輝史によるデザイン事務所。社名のコンセプトは、2D＝平面デザインと3D＝空間デザインの掛け合いによって生み出されるものを求めて6Dとした。いろいろなアウトプットの表現ができると考え、一つのロゴデザインに固執せず、あえて2種のロゴを制作。エコバッグやTシャツは、来社してくれた人へプレゼントすることで、コミュニケーションの一端を担っている。

A design office belonging to graphic designer, Shogo Kishino, and space designer, Terufumi Otsubo. The concept of the office name 6D comes from the idea of a cross between the 2D of graphic design and the 3D of space design. Instead of the usual single logo, two different logos have been produced to express the idea that the company is capable of various types of output. An eco-bag and a T-shirt serve as communication tools and are presented to visitors to the office.

Japan　AD, D: 木住野彰悟　Shogo Kishino　DF, S: ロクディ　6D

ポスター Poster.

ジョット・グラフィカ　Giottographica

![Giottographica®]

2002年、いのうえよしひろ + yukinkoにより設立。CDジャケット、ロゴ、ファッションカタログ、グッズ、広告等を中心に、アートディレクション、撮影ディレクション、デザイン、イラストレーション、撮影小道具作成までトータルに活動。代表作は木村カエラ、吉井和哉、いきものがかり、フジファブリックなど。社名ロゴのコンセプトは、「シンプルで視認性のよい固まり」。自社ツールは名刺、封筒、レターヘッド、紙袋、ガムテープ、会社案内等。封筒には白の箔押し加工、テープは封筒との相性を考慮し「紙」を素材に選んでいる。

A design unit created by Yoshihiro Inoue and yukinko that deals mainly in the design of CD inserts, logos, promotional goods and advertising but also provides a comprehensive range of design services from art direction, design, illustration and production of photographic props. The concept for the company's logo is a "simple, highly visible block of text." Giottographica's business tools consist of business cards, envelopes, letterhead, paper bags, masking tape, and a company profile. The envelopes underwent a white foiling process and paper was chosen as the material for the masking tape because of its affinity with the envelopes.

Japan　　AD, D: いのうえよしひろ Yoshihiro Inoue / yukinko　　DF, S: ジョット・グラフィカ Giottographica

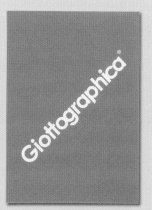

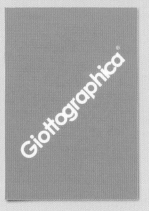

ステッカー Sticker

ライター Lighter

キーホルダー Key Ring

プロモーションキット Promotion Kit

canaria

カナリア　canaria

クリエイティブエージェンシー
Creative Agency

徳田祐司が2007年に設立したコミュニケーションデザインカンパニー。社名は「身体は小さくても、舞台は世界へ」という想いを込めてつけられた。コーポレートカラーは、カナリアの和名である「金糸雀」から、カナリアイエローと金色に。名刺もカナリアということを意識し、少し小さめのサイズとした。封筒はオリジナルの黄色いものを1種制作し、送る相手や郵便物の内容によってステッカーの種類を変えて貼る仕様に。これらのツールも、周囲とのコミュニケーションを図ることに重きをおいて制作した。

A communication design company established in 2007 by Yuji Tokuda. The company name incorporates the idea that "We may be small but the world is our stage." The corporate colors are canary yellow and gold. The business cards were made a little smaller than usual to evoke the idea of a small canary bird. Only one type of envelope, in yellow, was produced, with a range of stickers that are used according to the addressee or the contents of the envelope. These business tools have been produced with an emphasis on encouraging communication with those around us.

Japan　CD, AD: 徳田祐司 Yuji Tokuda　D: 山崎万梨子 Mariko Yamasaki / 藤井幸治 Kouji Fujii　Manager: 清水英理子 Eriko Shimizu　DF, S: カナリア　canaria

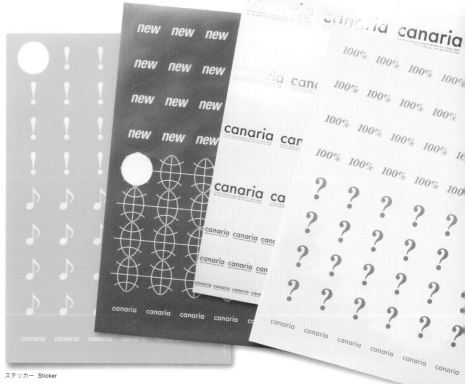

ステッカー　Sticker

設立案内 Establishment Invitation

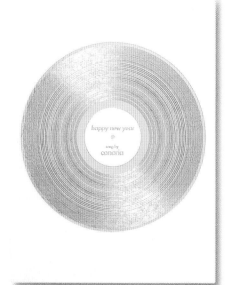

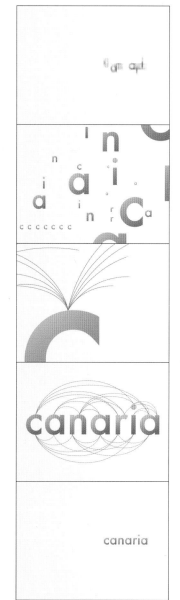

年賀状 New Year Card

サウンドロゴ Sound Logo

goen°

アートディレクター・森本千絵を中心に、2007年に設立されたデザイン事務所。「出会いを発明する。夢をカタチにし、人をつなげていく」というコンセプトのもと、屋号を「ご縁」=「goen」とした。自社ツールには、スタンダード名刺とパラパラ漫画となっているアニメイシ、オープニングパーティで配られたオリジナルコイン等。人と人とのつながりを大切にする同社のコンセプトのように、どのツールにも関わる人が楽しめるアイデアが取り入れられている。オフィスは、部屋の中に小屋が建てられている設計とし、あたたかみのある世界観を体現できる空間となっている。

Design office led by art director Chie Morimoto, established in 2007. Based on a concept of "inventing encounters, making dreams real and connecting people" the company was named "goen" meaning "connection". The company's promotional tools include standard business cards and "anime-shi" cards in flip comic form, and the original coins distributed at the opening party. In accordance with the company's emphasis on connections between people, every tool incorporates ideas that those involved will enjoy. The offices take the form of "huts" built in a room, spaces that embody a warm, welcoming view of the world.

Japan   CD, AD, D: 森本千絵 Chie Morimoto   DF,S: goen°

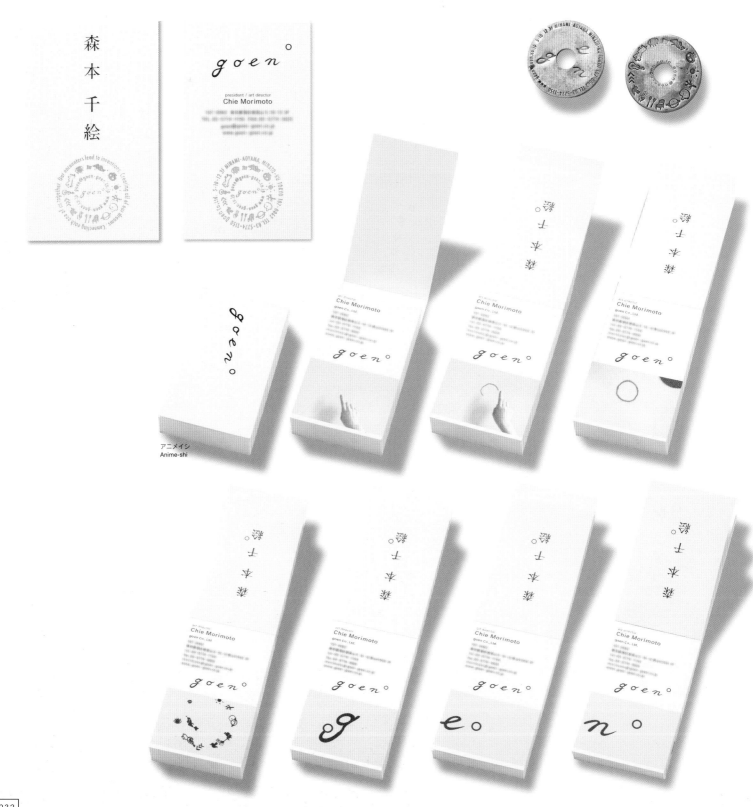

アニメイシ
Anime-shi

dreamdesign

ドリームデザイン　dreamdesign co., ltd.

クリエイティブエージェンシー
Creative Agency

クリエイティブディレクター・石川淳哉が代表をつとめるクリエイティブエージェンシー。会社のコンセプトは「夢はカタチにできる」。社名の「dream」と「design」は、想像と実現、やわらかな発想と強い意志、という思いをそれぞれ表現している。名刺、封筒などの自社ツールは、受け取った人が手にした瞬間からコミュニケーションが拡がるようなユニークで個性のあるデザインとなっている。なお、同社は2008年に10周年を迎えた際、記念のカードや年賀状もオリジナルで制作している。

A creative agency represented by creative director Junya Ishikawa, with the concept "your dreams can become a reality." The words "dream" and "design" in the company's name respectively express imagination and materialization, and soft ideas teamed with strong determination. The company's distinctive business tools such as the business cards and envelopes are designed to communicate from the moment they are placed in someone's hands. The company also produced its own commemorative cards and New Year cards on the occasion of its tenth anniversary in 2008.

Japan　　CD: 石川淳哉 Junya Ishikawa　　AD: 岩井博文 Hirofumi Iwai　　D: 日置好文 Yoshifumi Hioki　　S: ドリームデザイン　dreamdesign co., ltd.

ステッカー
Sticker

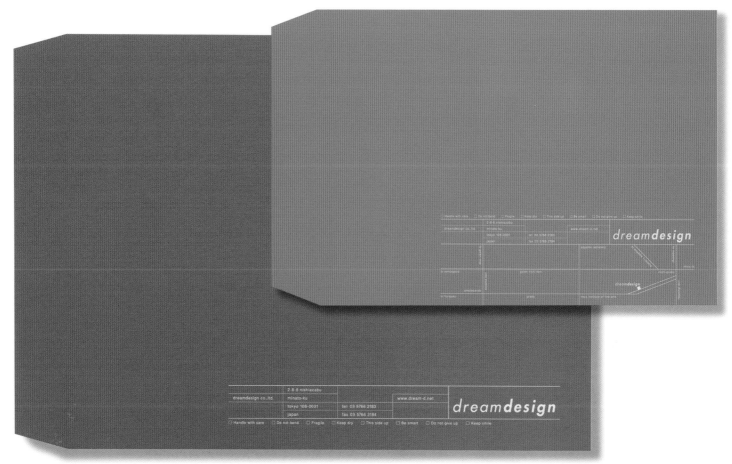

ニューイヤーの期間限定ウェブサイト　Special Web Site for New Year

年賀状　New Year Card

Three & Co. 3

スリーアンドコー　Three & Co.

クリエイティブディレクター・福森正紀を中心とした、グラフィック広告やパッケージ、ウェブデザイン等を主に制作するデザイン会社。社名のThree(3)は、2次元の媒体だけにとらわれず、世の中に存在するすべての物(3次元)のデザインにチャレンジする、という意志を掲げている。社名のロゴは、限りなくフラットでナチュラルな書体を採用。飽きが来ず、長く使えるロゴにすることによって、時代やコンセプトの進化にも対応できるものとなっている。ツールは名刺、封筒、シールなどで、それぞれに箔押しやシルク印刷などの特殊加工が施されている。

A design company headed by Masaki Fukumori that produces mainly graphic advertising, as well as packaging and website design. The numeral 3 in the name shows a desire to accept the challenge expressing the three dimensions of everything that exists in the world within a two-dimensional medium. The logo for the company's name uses a flat, natural typeface. Creating a logo that can be used for a long time without people tiring of it means that it can be adapted to the constantly changing times and concepts. The company's business tools that include business cards, envelope and stickers have all undergone special foiling and silkscreen printing processes.

Japan　CD, AD, D: 福森正紀 Masaki Fukumori　DF, S: スリーアンドコー Three & Co.

封筒　Envelope

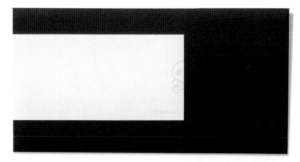

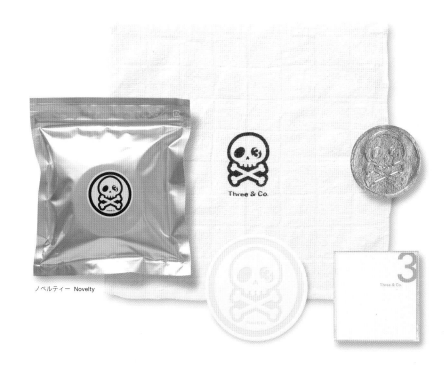

ノベルティー Novelty

ノート Notebook

&&&

イギリスに所在する&&&は広告とアートの分野で活躍するクリエイティブエージェンシー。実験的で独創的なスタイルはオフィスステーショナリーやツールにも見受けられる。DVDは作品をアーカイブ、ドキュメンテーションするデジタルポートフォリオとして社内外で活用。ウェブサイトではデザイナーの顔と制作工程を紹介している。

&&& is a UK based creative agency working in both commercial and art sector. Office stationeries and tools well capture the agency's creativity and experimental design. DVD is a digital portfolio used internally and externally to archive and document agency's work. Website invites viewers to meet designers and watch work being produced.

UK   CD: Simon Brown   D: Shawn Davey   DF, S: &&&

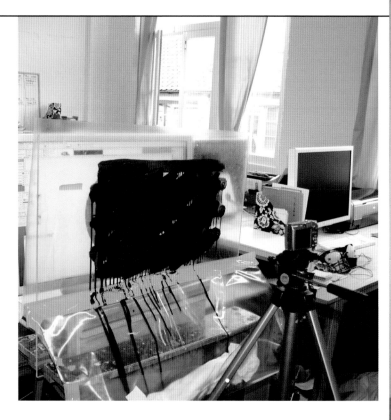

ウェブサイト Web Site

intégral ruedi baur

intégral ruedi baur paris
5 rue jules vallès f-75011 paris
t. 0033 01 55 25 81 10 f. 0033 01 43 48 08 07
atelier@irb-paris.eu www.irb-paris.eu

パリを拠点にチューリッヒとベルリンにもオフィスを持つグラフィックデザイン事務所intégral reudi baur。名刺の表には作品を用い、裏面には名前や住所などの個人情報が印刷ではなく個々のスタンプで捺印されたユニークなもの。その他のツールはカラーバリエーション豊富で、社内用、社外用として使われている。

Integral Ruedi Baur is a graphic design office with branches in Paris, Zurich and Berlin. On one side of the business card shows project work and on the reverse side personal information such as name and email address are stamped on (not printed) by individual inking pad. Other office tools come in variety of colors created for internal and external use.

France   DF, S: intégral ruedi baur

chantal grossen
intégral ruedi baur paris
5 rue jules vallès f-75011 paris
+33.1 55 25 81 10 www.irb-paris.eu
chgrossen@irb-paris.eu

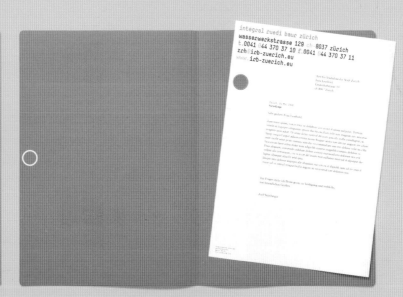

KK Outlet

アムステルダムに所在するKK Outletは広告、商品開発、デザインそして出版を手がけるコミュニケーションエージェンシー。オフィススペースの中にデザインショップとギャラリーも展開している。オフィスにショップとギャラリーを融合したKK Outletのユニークなコンセプトは、シンプルなグラフィックに赤と青で統一されたロゴ、そしてオフィスステーショナリーのデザインにも表れている。

KK Outlet based in Amsterdam is a communications agency with a shop and a gallery combined in one office. Field of work covers advertising, product development, design and publishing. This unique concept of multifunctional office with a combined shop, gallery and workspace is reflected in the KK Outlet's logo and stationary design - the simple graphics and the use of blue and red colors help support KK Outlet's ad hoc attitude.

Netherlands   CD, AD: Eric Kessels   D: Anthony Burrill   P: Timothy Soar   DF, S: Kesselskramer

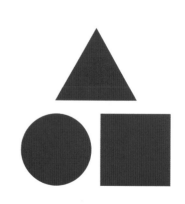

ステッカー Sticker

カード Card

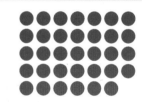

KK OUTLET
FALAFEL
DOLPHIN MEAT
COMMUNICATION
BOOKS
CUFFLINKS
ART
KesselsKramer London 42 Hoxton Square London N1 6PB Tel +44(0)207 033 7680 Fax +44(0)207 739 0396 www.kkoutlet.com

DVD

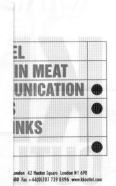

KK OUTLET

KK OUTLET

KK OUTLET

YOU ARE:
INVITED
PROVOKED
SCARED
DISGUSTED

TO ATTEND:
A SERVICE STATION
KK OUTLET
THE LAUNDROMAT
HARDWARE SHOP

AT:
42 HOXTON SQUARE
12 WHITES ROW
LAURIERGRACHT 39
41 WHITCOMB STREET

ON:
SATURDAY JUNE 14th 2008 9.00PM
FRIDAY FEBRUARY 1st 2008 7.00PM
FRIDAY DECEMBER 25th 2009 5.00AM
FRIDAY JANUARY 1st 2010 1.00AM

FOR:
MASSAGE
DUTCH LESSONS
DRINKS
BURLESQUE DANCING

BECAUSE:
YOU OWE US MONEY
YOUR HAIR SMELLS NICE
IT'S OUR OPENING
YOU'VE GOT THE KEYS

rsvp@kkoutlet.com KesselsKramer London 42 Hoxton Square London N1 6PB Tel +44(0)207 033 7680 www.kkoutlet.com

DM

KK OUTLET

Sagmeister Inc.

Sagmeister Inc.はニューヨークに拠点を置くデザイン事務所、デザイナーStefan Sagmeisterが創立。ポスター、カタログ、出版物、アイデンティティーからパッケージング、CDカバーなど印刷物全般のデザインを手がける。スライドして開く名刺はアセテートプラスチックを使用、傾けると文字が見え隠れする作りとなっている。

Sagmeister Inc. is a graphic design company in New York City, founded by Stefan Sagmeister. The company design all things printed, from posters, brochures, books and annual reports to identity systems, perfume packaging and CD cover. Business card that slides open is made of acetate plastic that reveals logo by angle.

USA   AD, D: Stefan Sagmeister   DF, S: Sagmeister Inc.

SAGMEISTER INC.

NEW YORK

封筒 Envelope

[TOM HINGSTON STUDIO]

Tom Hingston Studio

クリエイティブエージェンシー
Creative Agency

音楽、ファッション、フィルム、モーショングラフィックス、広告やブランディングとマルチに手がけるTom Hingston Studioは、ロンドンに所在するデザインエージェンシー。落ち着きのあるすっきりとしたデザインとは対照的なテクスチャーのある紙に、様々な印刷方法で加工されたオフィスステーショナリーは、触感のある仕上がりとなっている。

Tom Hingston Studio is an independent multi-disciplinary design agency, based in London. Field of work covers music, fashion, film, motion graphics, advertising and branding. The design of the office stationary was intended to be both pure and understated, this was then contrasted with the use of textured paper stocks and different print finishes to give each item a tactile quality.

UK   CD, AD, D, DF, S: Tom Hingston Studio

カード Card

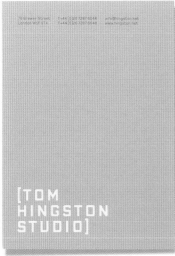

ステッカー Sticker

SÄGENVIER

クリエイティブエージェンシー
Creative Agency

オーストリアに所在するSÄGENVIERはグラフィックデザイン、インフォーメーションデザイン、コミュニケーションデザインを手がけるデザインスタジオ。デザインの多くに見られる数字の4はスタジオが位置する道路の番地「Sagerstrasse 4」から来ている。オフィスステーショナリーには型押し、エンボス加工、手作りスタンプなど様々な技法が用いられている。

SÄGENVIER is a design studio based in Austria whose field of work includes graphic design, information design and communication design. Use of number 4 in many of the design originates from the street address "Sagerstrasse 4" where the studio is located. Office stationeries are played with different style and technique such as imprinting, embossing, and handmade stamps.

Austria   CD, AD, D: Sigi Ramoser   D: Klaus Österle   DF, S: SÄGENVIER

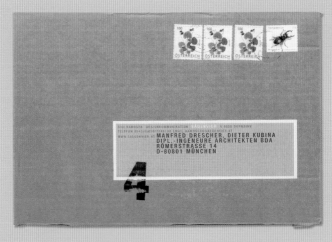

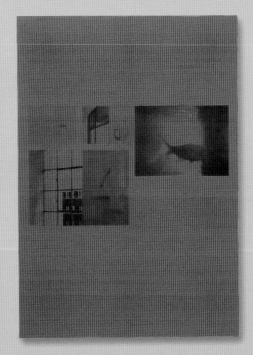

会社案内 Company Brochure

MO

MOはロンドンとパリに所在するデザインエージェンシー。ロゴはグラフィカルなデザインに仕上げている。オフィスステーショナリーの書体にはFutura MediumとPrestige Eliteを用い、厚紙にステンシル印刷を施している。

MO is a London-Paris based design agency. Logotype designed in a graphical manner and accompanied with Futura Medium and Prestige Elite. Stationary is stencil printed on a bulky paper.

France   D, S: Kasia Korczak   D: David Bennewith

ステッカー Sticker

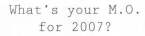

What's your M.O.
for 2007?

Michael +31(0)6 1672 3891
Oriane +33(0)6 0717 2663

Email info@mocreatives.com
www.mocreatives.com

New Year's Resolutions:
branding, graphics,
music, new media
products, animations,
events...

das
kapital
hill

Michael +31(0)6 1672 3891
Oriane +33(0)6 0717 2663

Email info@mocreatives.com
www.mocreatives.com

New Year's Resolutions:
branding, graphics,
music, new media
products, animations,
events...

年賀状 New Year Card

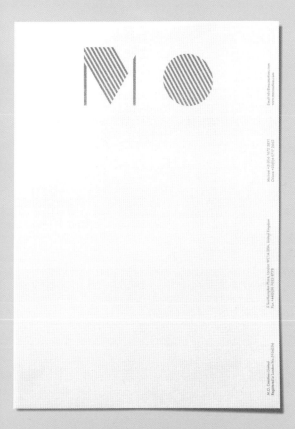

年賀状 New Year Card

WORK Architecture Company

Work Architecture Companyはニューヨークに所在する建築事務所。形にとらわれない流動的な仕事をする会社として、ロゴは常に変形するグラフィックの中に社名が入ったデザイン。500種類あるロゴのうち100種類がオフィスステーショナリーに採用され、このうち12種類が名刺に使われている。また便箋には異なったロゴがレーザー印刷され、アニメーションされたロゴもあり、プレゼンテーションやレクチャー映像に使われている。

WORK Architecture Company is based in New York. To emphasize the fluid nature of the practice, logo is a graphic system that combines a static logotype with a constantly shifting graphic mark. Out of 500 logo forms, 100 were picked for the stationeries. Business cards come in 12 different logo forms. Each letterhead is laser-printed and features a randomly chosen logo, and there is also an animated version of the logo used in presentation and lecture materials.

USA   CD: Prem Krishnamurthy / Adam Michaels   D: Chris McCaddon / Justin Smith / Mary Voorhees / Sam Gray   DF, S: Project Projects

WORK ARCHITECTURE COMPANY
156 LUDLOW STREET 3RD FLOOR NY NY 10002
T 212 228 1333 F 212 228 1674
WWW.WORK.AC

FRED AWTY
FRED@WORK.AC
M 646 637 5887

Brighten the Corners

Brighten the Corners

イギリス・ロンドンとドイツ・シュツットガルトにオフィスを持つBrighten the Corners はデザイン全般と企画戦略を専門とするデザインエージェンシー。同社のロゴは従来の「ロゴ」として扱わず、言葉の意味を伝えるために「キャプション」として常に写真や文字、イラストと共に見せるようにしている。

Brighten the Corners is an independent, multi-disciplined design and strategy consultancy with offices in London and Stuttgart. Logo designed as a caption rather than a traditional logo, the mark always appears alongside photography, type of illustration in the office tools making full use of its descriptive name.

UK   D: Billy Kiossoglou   D: Frank Philippin   DF, S: Brighten the Corners

April showers bring May flowers.

Brighten the Corners
Unit 243, The Bon Marché Centre
241-251 Ferndale Road, London SW9 8BJ
Telephone +44 (0)20 7274 4949
Lindenspürstraße 32, D-70176 Stuttgart
Telephone +49 (0)711 3 05 68 31
frank@brightenthecorners.com
Mobile +49 (0)160 5536 117

Prof. Frank Philippin MA RCA

The darker the night, the nicer the day.

Rain before seven, fine for eleven.

Count on a good weather day, if it starts out foggy grey.

バッジ Badge

welcome!
let's turn on the light
of the world!
get with the times!
sing along!

COMA

ニューヨークとアムステルダムにオフィスを持つクリエイティブエージェンシー。印刷物からインスタレーションまでのアートディレクション、デザイン、制作を手がける。「どの出逢いにも色がある」というコンセプトの下、友人やクライアント向けのギフトとして作られたカラーカードの封筒の内側には、1年間に出会った人々の名前とその人に充てた色が、その人の言語で書かれている。自社用広告ポスターは、デザインへの見識を作品と共に説明している。砂糖箱には、「あなたにとって甘さとは?」という問いに答えた120人の手書きの答えが印刷された角砂糖が入っている。

COMA, a creative agency with offices in New York and Amsterdam, art directs, designs and produces various works from print, Internet to installations. Color cards, as a gift to friends and clients, the inside of the envelope list all the names of people encountered in 2001, each person given a color name in their language. Promotional ads show an image of a project worked on with a verb and an explanation achieved in the work. Sugar box contains 120 cubes with answers to the question of "describe something sweet" asked to various people, printed in their handwriting.

USA   CD, AD, DF, S: COMA Amsterdam / New York

COMA

CORNELIA BLATTER

COMA@AYA.YALE.EDU
WWW.COMA-LIVE.COM

121 DOBBIN STREET #6
BROOKLYN NY 11222 USA
T (+1) 718 349 9783
F (+1) 718 349 9783

COMA

MARCEL HERMANS

COMA@AYA.YALE.EDU
WWW.COMA-LIVE.COM

SAXENBURGERSTRAAT 21-1
1054 KN AMSTERDAM NL
T +31 (0)20 692 8277
F +31 (0)20 692 3659

every encounter has a color.
iridescent white for kate, sneeuwwit voor valentine, bleach blond for andrea, parelwit voor renny, amber white for beth, almond for craig, titanium white for duane, chroom voor rem, edelweiss for sandra, zilver voor sonja, ivory white for suzanne, champagne voor teo, blanc de titane pour jean-babtist, ivoor voor fieke, kanariegeel voor cisca, reichbleichgold für gaby, bri.... yellow for hana, gold für hebi, lichtend zonnegeel voor jantje, safraangeel voor jeannine, oxidgelb für jens, ochre for kim, goudgeel voor krijn, zonnebloemg... ...s geel voor maartje, vanille geel voor madeleine, mosterdgeel voor misha, goldocker für patricia, naples yellow hue for penny, rotgold für rolf, ...yellow for sally, goldgelb für trudi, ocker für werner, satijngoud voor wout, kadmiumoranje voor frits, dessert orange for will, tang... ...tongerine for judith, cognac voor sebastiaan, fluorescent orange for laurie, blueish orange or pink green for burkhard, fluori.... ...enrood voor ernestine, eggplant for grant, plumred for leslie, kanarierood voor marijn, scarf red for bernard, ker... ...milioenrood voor jurgen, rouche de pompéi pour fabienne, krapprot für andrea, kardinaalrood voor fr... ...ina, carravagiorood voor marten, hamburger steinrot für hadi, steenrood voor jan, aard... ...y, himbeer...ot für susanne, carravagio red for julia, crimson for kristin, rosso por ... ...iek, bloed...ood voor lucette, karminrot für maria, carmine red for april, karmijnro... ...purple red for paola, erdbeerrot für szilvia, wine red for susanna, magenta voor maa... ...ed for margit, indian red for uschi, akari red for douglas, mauve for christopher ... ...chsia for vito, aubergine for john, roze voor eef, 87% magenta voor freek, mang... ...ink ...arnation for kayhan, vivid lavender for jessica, flamingoroze voor katja... ...e voor rick, light peach for theodora, old rose for fred, horizon blue for claris... ...iesblauw voor margriet, eisblau für dominik, kobaltblau für joerg, glanzend... ...or barbara, zilverblauw voor bert, denimblauw voor carl, ocean blue for deeni... ...voor ineke, hemelblauw voor floris, pale blue for gabriel, navy blue fo... ...canary blue for helga, prussian blue for katura, schimmerndes schme... ...pruisischblauw voor jaap, bleu de céruléum pour jacques, mitternac... ...tblue for joseph, indigo for mark, bertblauw voor karin, salvia blue... ...für bice, delfsblauw voor frederieke, alpineblauw voor maya, turqu... ...eladon for avo, maagdenpalmblauw voor barbera, kobaltblauw voor... ...oor rutger, azure blue for jodi, steel blue for sarah, ultramarinblau fü... ...awrence, light blue for steve, dunkelblau for anke, staalblauw voor su... ...reen for roger, woudgroen voor ernst, jungle green for ayumi, pine green fo... ...r hans-ulrich, brilliant green for ed, lettuce green for greg, mint green fo... ...n feurig für markus, venetian green for michael, mistletoe green for peter, cana... ...ve green for kristjan, waldgrün für jacqueline, lime green for jennifer, calypso g... ...own for martin, gebrande sienna voor christine, oxidbraun für marco, reebruin vo... ...or auke, olivbraun für kai, sandalwood for linda, pms 877 for jason, antraciet vo... ...e gray for christoph, grüngrau für gereon, luminous silver for frank, donkergroen voor bas, hellgrau für stefan, lampzwart voor... ...kayhan, jet black for tom, perlschwarz für christoph, eisenoxidschwarz für michael, ijzeroxidezwart voor donald, parelzwart voor anthon... ...n for bruce, luminous black for jennifer, shiny black for susan and all colors of the rainbow for judith. every encounter has a color.
coma, cornelia blatter & marcel hermans

カード Card

砂糖箱 Sugar Box

CLICK:

[to totally groove with a client]

www.comalive.com

TRUST IN THINGS THAT DON'T FIT

www.comalive.com

TICKLE:

[to wiggle your finger under someone's armpits until you get a reaction. (it's the reaction that counts)]

www.comalive.com

SPLICE:

[to edit, juxtapose]

www.comalive.com

[let your mind go blank for a moment] · · · · · · · · · · · and free associate with "swiss" · · · · · · · SWISS · · · · · · · · What do you think of? · · · · · · · · (Let me guess) · · · · · · · · · Swiss Miss · · · · · · · swiss watches · · · · · · · · · swiss Army knife · · · · · the swiss grid · · · · · · · · What have they all got in common? · · · · · · · · mm-hmmm · · · · that's right · · · · · · · · · precision · · · · · · · (enough said)

SWISSIFY:

[to alter the nature of something by making it excruciatingly precise]

www.comalive.com

TRANSLATE:

[to take any old idea and communicate it differently]

www.comalive.com

ポスター Poster

STILETTO NYC

印刷物全般とビデオのアートディレクションを手がけるSTILETTO NYCはニューヨークとミラノにオフィスを持つデザインスタジオ。自社プロモーションツールとして作られたStilettoポスターは新しい作品を紹介するDVDと共に送られたもの。この他、過去の作品を集めたSTILETTOポスターシリーズ（本にまとめて出版する予定）や、クリスマスプレゼントとして得意先に送られた、ロゴの刺繍が美しいウール製スカーフなども制作している。

STILETTO NYC is a design studio based in New York and Milan, that specializes in art direction & design for print and video. Stiletto poster is a self-promotional tool sent out together with a DVD to spread the word about the new work. Stiletto poster series are work printed and collected over the years, eventually to be published as a collection. Stiletto holiday scarves, made in wool with a beautiful embroidered stiletto logo, were sent to clients as a holiday gift.

USA / Italy   CD, AD, D, DF, S: STILETTO NYC

OSHIMA inc.

大島事務所　Oshima inc.

広告のアートディレクションやアパレルのグラフィック、CDジャケットのディレクション等、幅広い分野で活動中のアートディレクター・大島慶一郎の個人事務所。自社ツールは名刺、封筒、DM。名刺と封筒はロゴマークのみを配置したシンプルなデザインに。DMは6種類あり、順に並べると自身の名前「OSHIMA」ができあがる仕組みとなっている。DMの基本ビジュアルである動植物は、誰からも愛され、癒しを与えてくれる身近な存在であるため、自分も仕事を通してそんな存在になれれば、という想いが込められている。

The private office of art director, Keiichiro Oshima, who is active in a wide range of fields including art direction for advertising, graphic design for the apparel industry and production of CD inserts. The company's business tools consist of business cards, envelopes and DM. The placing of the logo only on the business cards and the envelopes has made for a simple overall design. There are six kinds of DM, which if lined up in order form the name Oshima. The DM features animals and plants as a means of conveying the company's wish to have the same cherished and calming presence in people's lives.

Japan　AD, D, I, S: 大島慶一郎　Keiichiro Oshima

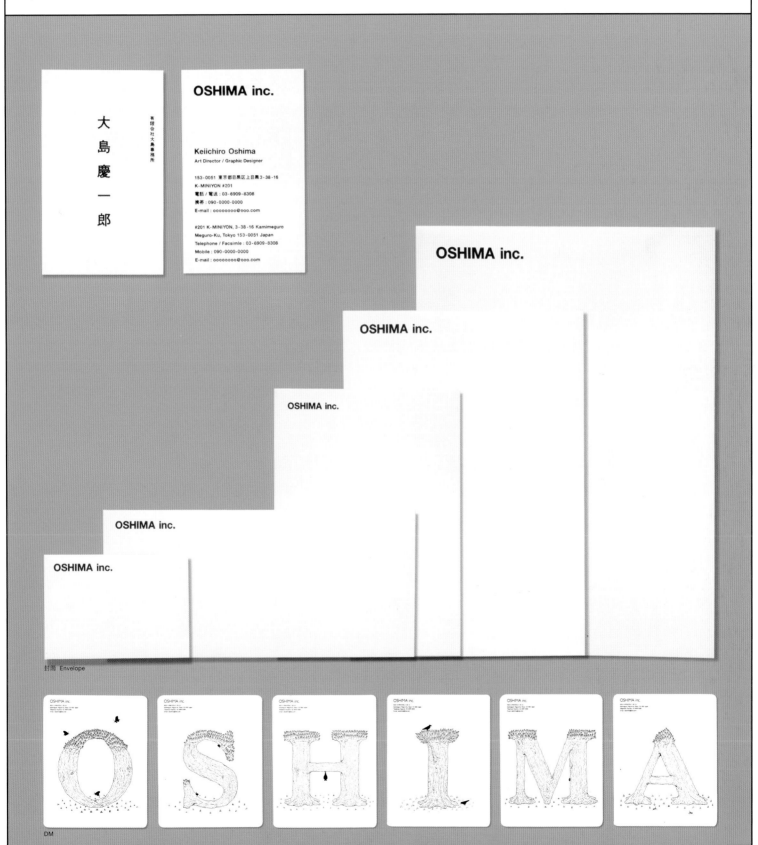

封筒 Envelope

DM

ボブファンデーション　Bob Foundation

朝倉充展と鈴木洋美の二人からなるクリエイティブグループ。親しみやすい名前にしたいという想いと、手を使って何かを作り出していきたいという想いから、人の名前である「Bob」と「Foundation」をつなげて事務所名とした。ロゴは、やわらかい印象を出すために手描きに。名刺の裏にはチェックボックスがついており、渡す相手によってメッセージを変えることができる。また、シルクスクリーンの作品を制作する際に余った紙を、事務所のツールとしても使用。ペーパーブランドNumber62では、オリジナルのラッピングペーパー等を発表している。

A creative group consisting of Mitsunori Asakura and Hiromi Suzuki. The office's name is based on the idea of combining a friendly-sounding name such as "Bob" with the word "foundation," meaning to create something with one's hands. The logo has been hand-drawn to achieve a soft finish. The back of the business cards has a range of different messages that can be ticked and then given to the card's recipient. The paper that was left over from silkscreen work has been used for the office's business tools. Some original wrapping papers among other things have also been released in paper brand Number62.

Japan　AD, D, DF, S: ボブファンデーション　Bob Foundation

daily press

デイリープレス　daily press

デイリープレスは、デザインやライフスタイルというカテゴリーを中心としたアタッシェ・ド・プレス事務所。モノ、コト、ヒトと国内外のジャーナリストとの間に密なコミュニケーションが生まれるよう、独自なスタイルで活動する。自社ツールのデザインはアートディレクター・山田信男（セントラルパーク）が担当した。直線と円弧からなる斜体のロゴタイプは「明るく軽快、楽しく元気」をイメージ。高白色で上質な紙に印刷された色鮮やかなデザインは、同社の爽やかで可愛らしい、前向きな様子が上手く表現されている。

Daily press is a press office with a focus on design and lifestyle. It operates with a style all its own in order to create close communication between the who, why, when and what on the one hand and Japanese and foreign journalists on the other. The design office Central Park, established by art director Nobuo Yamada, was responsible for the productions of the company's business tools. The logo, which is based on the ideas of "bright, light-hearted, healthy and active," is in a vivid green. The white and bright blue envelopes cleverly communicate the way the company is fresh and cute and forward-moving.

Japan　AD, D: 山田信男 Nobuo Yamada / 田部井美奈 Mina Tabei (Logo Mark)　DF, S: セントラルパーク　CENTRAL PARK

KOBAYASHI DESIGN STUDIO

小林デザインスタジオ　KOBAYASHI DESIGN INC.

リフォームを中心とした建築デザインを手がけている建築会社。ロゴデザインおよび自社ツールは、広告代理店・東急エージェンシーが手がけている。ロゴデザインは、「KOBAYASHI DESIGN INC.」の頭文字の「K」をデザイン化したもの。自社ツールは名刺、封筒の他、会社設立案内のDMがある。社名が楽しげに伝わることをコンセプトに、全面に絵柄のある封筒と社員の名刺をつなげてみると、一枚の絵ができあがるという、とてもユニークな仕掛けが施されたツールとなっている。

An architectural firm that deals in architectural design with a focus on remodelling. The logo design and the company's business tools were handled by the advertising agency, Tokyu Advertising Agency Co. Ltd. The logo design features the initial letter "K" in the name Kobayashi Design Inc. The company's business tools consist of business cards, envelopes as well as DM with information on the company's establishment. As a way of advertising the company name in a fun way, the envelopes that are covered in a pattern and the staff business cards when joined together form a picture, an extremely unique device for enhancing the business tools.

Japan　CD: 明富士治郎 Jiro Akefuji　AD, D: 池澤 樹 Tatsuki Ikezawa　CW: 中里智史 Satoshi Nakazato　I: 日野俊臣 Shunjin Hino　S: 東急エージェンシー Tokyu Agency Inc.

DM

レバン　LEVAN inc.

グラフィックデザイン・TV-CM制作を中心としたデザイン事務所。マークのコンセプトは「草原」。草原はとても自由で、柔軟に形を変えるとてもクリエイティブな存在であると考え、「デザイン業界の大草原を目指す」としている。ロゴは、会社のコンセプトである草原をモチーフにしたもので、LEVANの頭文字である「L」を地平線としてとらえたデザイン。レターヘッドを除く、すべての自社ツールを横につなげてみると長い長い草原ができあがり、これらのツールは社のコンセプトを反映したデザインで統一している。

A graphic design office headed by creative director Junya Kamada, based on the concept of "the prairie." Kamada believes that the expansive and constantly changing prairie is a creative entity and presents Levan as the great prairie of the design industry. The logo takes the company's prairie concept as a motif, and the letter "L" in the company's name serves as the design's horizon. Align the edges of all of Levan's business tools, with the exception of the letterhead, and you can see the expansive prairie that unifies the tools and reflects the company's concept.

Japan　CD, AD, D: 鎌田順也 Junya Kamada　D: 宇部信也 Shinya Ube / 佐々木大輔 Daisuke Sasaki　I: 佐藤正樹 Masaki Sato　DF, S: レバン LEVAN inc.

封筒 Envelope

DESIGN BOY Inc.

螢光TOKYOのデザインオフィスとして2006年に設立。「デザインの厨房として、少年のようにデザインに遊び心を持って創作する」がコンセプト。ロゴは、格好をつけたデザインよりも遊び心のあるデザインを心がけ、筆文字の書体を用いて、赤、青、黄色の三原色でデザインの原点を意識している。自社ツールは名刺、封筒、紙袋、会社案内。名刺には、ロゴ部分にバーコ印刷を採用し、立体的な質感を表現した。また、封筒類は斜めから見ることによりDESIGN BOYのロゴが見えてくるという仕掛けが施されている。

A design office established in the main by Shin Orishige in 2006. Its concept is "a design kitchen for creating with the same sense of fun we had as children." The idea for the logo is a design with a sense of fun in mind rather than design that merely looks good, and using a brush-script typeface, it contains an awareness of the origin of the design with the primary colors of red, blue and yellow. The company business tools consist of business cards, envelopes, paper bags and a company profile. The raised thermography printing was used for the business cards. If you look at the stationery at an angle, the characters appear to be rising up off the surface.

Japan   CD: 螢光TOKYO KEI-KO TOKYO   AD, D, DF, S: DESIGN BOY

CENTRAL PARK

セントラルパーク　CENTRAL PARK

セントラルパークは、アートディレクター・山田信男が「人が集い楽しいことがはじまる、公園みたいなデザイン事務所」をコンセプトに設立。その名の通り、公園をイメージしたというオフィスの窓からは、東京とは思えない緑の風景が広がっている。自社ツールは、どれも山田氏が目指す「潔く美しいデザイン」でありながら、随所に遊び心が見え隠れする。名前が黒一色で印刷されたシンプルな名刺は、裏返すと銀色の文字の上にブランドカラーである蛍光黄緑を差し色に使用した、公園の陽だまりを思わせる柔かなデザインになっている。

A design office set up by art director, Nobuo Yamada with his concept of "beautiful, clean design." The company name encapsulates the idea of "a design office that resembles a park where people gather and things happen." The company's business tools, which embody that idea, are all of a beautiful and refined design at the same time as having an obvious sense of fun. Turn over the business cards where the name has been simply produced in the one color of black and see the soft design reminiscent of a park drenched in sunlight, using the fluorescent yellow green that is the color of the brand.

Japan　　AD, D: 山田信男 Nobuo Yamada　　DF, S: セントラルパーク　CENTRAL PARK

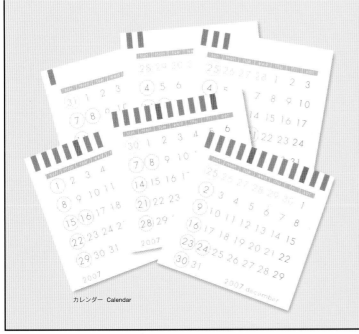

カレンダー　Calendar

COIL

コイル　COIL inc.

CI、VIの企画・デザイン制作などを手掛けるデザイン事務所。その場限りの利益を求めるのではなく、クライアントの本質を捉えて、利益と同等に文化発展につながる仕事をしていくことをコンセプトとしている。ロゴは、会社名のようにコイル状に巻き上がっていくようなイメージで制作。封筒は素材を布にしてハンコを使うことで、毎回違ったデザインを提供できる仕組みとなっている。ラフなどを書き込める「落書蝶」は、あえてムラのある、色落ちする印刷に。社名変更の際にコイル型のDMを制作するなど、各ツールがアイデアに溢れたデザインとなっている。

A design office dealing in CI and VI planning and design production and other design services. Its concept is not to focus on the ad hoc making of profit but rather to capture the essential quality of its clients and produce work that leads to cultural development alongside the making of profit. Inspired by the company name, the logo is designed in the shape of a coil. The envelopes have been made from cloth and are then stamped so that a different design can be presented each time. The sketchpad has a deliberately flawed look and printed so as to appear discolored. The coil-shaped DM was produced at the time the company changed its name.

Japan　DF, S: コイル　COIL inc.

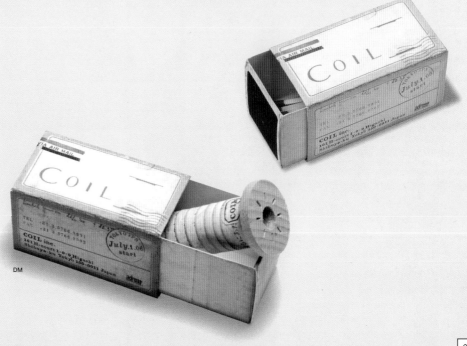

落書蝶

'06

ラクガキ ショウ

ノート Notebook

DM

UCHU COUNTRY

宇宙カントリー　Uchu Country

アートディレクター、映像ディレクターの野田 凪が主宰。LGのCMやCoca-ColaワールドキャンペーンのCM、フランスのデパートMONOPRIXのCMを手がけるなど、国内外で幅広く活躍している。名刺の裏面は、それぞれの絵柄が異なるデザインに。ハンパンダの生みの親でもあり、ぬいぐるみ、ステッカー、キーホルダーなど様々なグッズを展開している。

クリエイティーブエージェンシー
Creative Agency

A design group led by art director and audio-visual director, Nagi Noda involved in a wide range of activity both in Japan and overseas including television commercials for the LG, Coca-Cola world campaign and the French department store MONOPRIX. The back of the business cards each has a different pattern. Uchu Country is the originator of the "half panda" character, and has developed a range of novelty goods including soft toys, stickers and key rings.

Japan　CD, AD: 野田 凪 Nagi Noda　S: 宇宙カントリー Uchu Country

ステッカー　Sticker

キーホルダー　Key Ring

カード　Card

ぬいぐるみ　Stuffed Toy

partizan

ロンドン、ロサンゼルス、ニューヨークそしてパリに事務所を構えるディレクター集団。ミッシェル・ゴンドリーやトラクターなど世界各国のディレクターが集い、ミュージックビデオ、CM、ショートフィルム、ブランディングなど幅広い分野で活躍している。野田 凪も所属。コーポレートカラーである紺と黄色を自社ツールにも効果的に用い、ひと目で同社のツールだということが認識できる、シンプルながらも印象的なデザインとなっている。

A director group with offices in London, Los Angeles, New York and Paris, where directors from various countries around the world assemble for music video, commercial, short film and branding projects. Dark blue and yellow, the corporate colors for the company's business tools, have been used to great effect, making them instantly recognizable. All in all a simple yet impressive design.

UK / USA / France   S: 宇宙カントリー Uchu Country

カード Card

DVD

グリッツデザイン　gritzdesigninc.

gritzdesigninc.

アートディレクター・日高英輝が設立したデザイン事務所。事務所名の「グリッツ」は、スラングで「男っぽい」、「気骨がある」などの意味がある。04年の事務所移転に伴い、心機一転の意を込めて青から赤へコーポレートカラーを変更。その象徴としてドアを赤にした。名刺・封筒などの赤い長方形ロゴは「WELCOME」の気持ちを込め、そのドアをモチーフとしている。コストと質感を重視し、封筒などの汎用物はクラフト紙を使用。ワークスペースは「風通しのいいファクトリー」をコンセプトに遮断性とヌケを考慮し、高さ140cmのパーテーションを採用している。

A design office established by art director, Eiki Hidaka. The company name "Gritz" is slang for courage or fortitude. When the company moved premises in 2004, the corporate color was changed from blue to red to match the red front door of the new offices. A motif of a red rectangle to resemble the door has also been placed on the company's business tools (business cards, envelopes) to serve as a logo. Kraft paper has been used for the envelopes to convey respect for the qualities of materials. Low partitions of approximately 140cm in height have been placed around the office, to create an open, airy work area.

UK / USA / France　　CD, D: 日高英輝 Eiki Hidaka　　D: 相田俊一 Shunichi Aita / 水野英樹 Hideki Mizuno / 木谷 史 Fumi Kitani / 竹林一成 Kazushige Takebayashi　　DF, S: グリッツデザイン gritzdesigninc.

株式会社 グリッツデザイン
〒107-0062 東京都港区南青山6-13-9 ANISE南青山2B
TEL.03-5766-2460　FAX.03-5766-2461
E-mail ooo@oooo.co.jp
ANISE BUILDING #2B, 6-13-9, MINAMI-AOYAMA,
MINATO-KU, TOKYO, JAPAN, 107-0062
TEL.+81-3-5766-2460 FAX.+81-3-5766-2461
E-mail ooo@oooo.co.jp

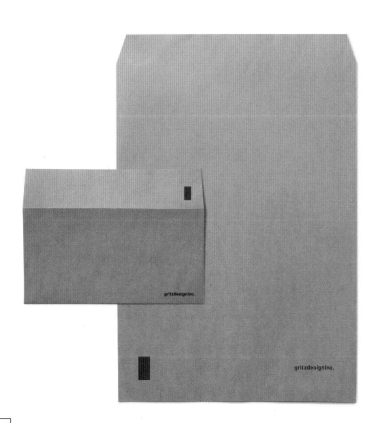

gritzdesigninc. anis minami-aoyama#29, 6-13-6, minami-aoyama, minato-ku, tokyo, japan, 107-0062 tel.03-5766-2460 fax.03-5766-2461

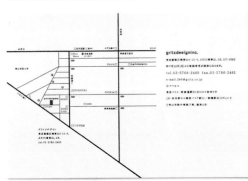

設立案内 Establishment Invitation

年賀状 New Year Card

アンテナグラフィックベース　antenna graphic base

アートディレクター・鷲見陽が設立したグラフィックデザイン事務所。ファッション、CDジャケットなど音楽関連のグラフィックを中心にCM、サインなども手がける。ロゴは、「ミラーボールの中にロゴが光っているのをイメージした」という、立体的で個性的なデザイン。自社ツールである名刺や封筒にもこのロゴがプリントされているが、モノトーンでありながらインパクトある仕上がりになっている。素っ気なくなりがちな封筒の裏にも小さなピースサインを入れるなど、ディテールにもこだわりが感じられる。

A graphic design office set up by art director, Akira Sumi, dealing mainly in graphic design for the fashion and music industries such as CD inserts, as well as commercials and signage. The logo has a unique three-dimensional design making the logo appear to be glittering inside a mirror ball. The logo is printed on the company's business cards and envelopes, which although monotone, has a strong impact. You can see the attention to detail in such things as the peace sign on the back of the understated envelopes.

Japan　AD, D: 鷲見 陽 Akira Sumi　DF, S: アンテナグラフィックベース　antenna graphic base

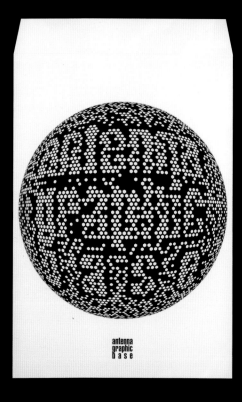

デイリー・フレッシュ　Dairy Fresh

広告、パッケージ、エディトリアル、CMなど、さまざまなジャンルを手がけるデザイン会社。また2007年より、同オフィスの一角でトートバッグとノートをはじめ、Tシャツ、キャップ、コインケースなどのオリジナルデザイングッズを販売するショップ「デイリー・フレッシュ・ストア」を運営している。自社ツールは名刺、封筒、紙袋。名刺の表面は、ホログラム箔をプレスした紙に名前、住所等を印刷している。オリジナルの紙袋は、アメリカのスーパーで使用されている質の悪い紙袋をイメージして制作している。

A design company involved in various genres such as advertising, packaging, editorial and commercials, plus since 2007 selling tote bags and notebooks as well as T-shirts, caps and coin cases from the corner of the office. The company's business tools consist of business cards, envelopes, paper bags. The person's name is printed on the front of the business card using pressed hologram foil. Dairy Fresh's paper bags are modelled on the low-quality paper bags found in American supermarkets.

Japan　CD, AD: 秋山具義 Gugi Akiyama　D: 加治真生子 Makiko Kaji　DF, S: デイリー・フレッシュ Dairy Fresh

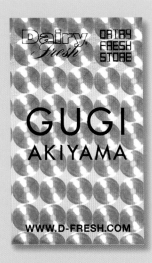

封筒 Envelope

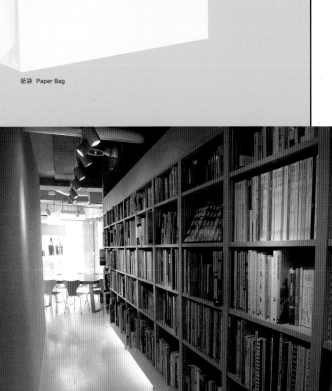

紙袋 Paper Bag

バタフライ・ストローク　butterfly・stroke inc.

広告の企画制作を中心に、制作者やキャラクターのマネージメント管理も行っているデザイン事務所。キャラクターデザインから、その展開やストーリー、造型までをトータルにディレクションし、新しいコンテンツを充実した表現で展開している。仕事で使う膨大な書類や資料を整理するためのツールはもちろん、トートバッグもサイズの細部にまでこだわるなど、使い勝手の良さを重視した造りとなっている。また、封筒用のシールはミシン目を入れ、開封しやすい工夫が施されている。

A design office that provides mainly advertising planning and production services but is also responsible for the management of producers and characters. It offers complete direction package from character design to their development, stories and creation of their shape and develops new content with comprehensive forms of expression. The business tools used for arranging the voluminous documents and materials used at work has naturally been designed for ease of use but there is also attention to detail in the sizing of the tote bag. The stickers for the envelopes have been perforated to make the envelopes easier to open.

Japan　CD, AD: 青木克憲 Katsunori Aoki　DF, S: バタフライ・ストローク butterfly・stroke inc.

ASYL

アジール ASYL

アートディレクター・佐藤直樹が主宰するデザイン事務所。音楽・映画・演劇・ファッション・出版・コンピュータ・通信等々、多種多様な業界と関わりを持ちながら、ジャンルを限定せず、企画・ディレクション・デザインをトータルに手がける。ロゴはシンプルで洗練された「かたち」にこだわりが感じられる。自社ツールは名刺、ステッカーなど。オリジナルの封筒はあえて作成せず、ステッカーを貼って使用。名刺の表面は各スタッフ色違い、裏面はメジウムインキを用いた活版印刷を採用している。

A design office headed by art director, Naoki Sato. ASYL has developed a diverse range of business interests including music, film, theatre, fashion, publishing, IT and communications, as well as offering planning, direction and design services that are not limited by genre. Its logo is simple and sophisticated with an emphasis on "form." The company's business tools include business cards and stickers. In a daring move, ASYL did not make its own envelopes, instead opting to use stickers on regular envelopes. The front of the business cards is in a different color for each staff member and the back has been letterpress printed with ink medium.

Japan　AD: 佐藤直樹 Naoki Sato　D: 溝端 貢 Mitsugu Mizobata　D: 坂脇 慶 Kei Sakawaki　DF, S: アジール ASYL

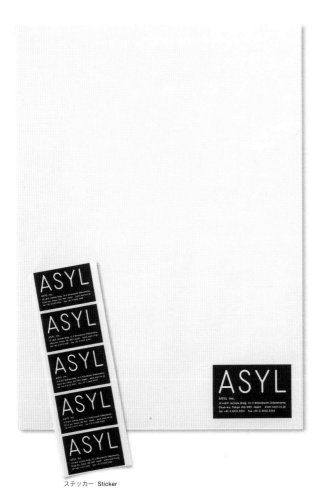

ステッカー Sticker

ANSWR

アンサー　ANSWR inc.

グラフィック集団ADAPTERを主宰する針谷建二郎により設立された、デザイン、メディア、ブランディング、マネージメントからなるクリエイティブスタジオ。〈純血〉ではなく〈混血〉のクリエイティビティこそが今の時代に適応した新しいコンセプトや美しい表現を生み出せる、という〈アイデンティティの混血〉がコンセプト。ロゴのコンセプトは「混血のクリエイティビティ」で、様々なフォントを混淆した。自社ツールは、組織を細かく分かりやすく記載するため、チェックボックスを使用したデザインフォーマットで構成されている。

A creative studio offering design, media, branding and management services established by Kenjiro Harigai who oversees the graphic design group ADAPTER. Its concept is one of the "blending of identity," where "blended" rather than "pure" creativity is capable of producing new concepts and beautiful forms of expression applicable to the times in which we live. ANSWR's logo is based on the concept of "blended creativity" and uses a mixture of different typefaces. Its business tools consist of a design format that uses check boxes to provide information about the organisation that is detailed yet easy to understand.

Japan　CD: 針谷建二郎 Kenjiro Harigai　AD: 内山尚志 Shoji Uchiyama　DF, S: アンサー　ANSWR inc.

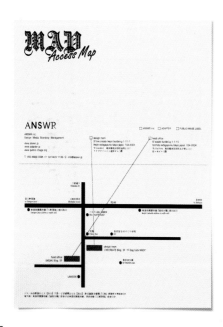
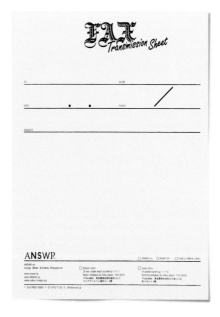
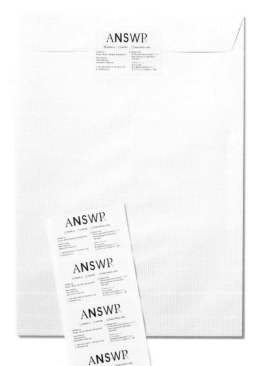

terashima design co.	**寺島デザイン制作室　Terashima Design Co.** グラフィックデザイナー・寺島賢幸によって1992年に設立されたグラフィックデザインスタジオ。ただ美しく見せるだけのデザインではなく、遊び心のある作品を特徴としている。自社ツールは名刺と封筒。名刺の裏面は全員共通だが、名前の入った面はデザイナーが各自でデザインをしているため、一人ひとりの名刺全てが異なった書体、異なったデザインとなっている。また、3枚の紙を合紙し、一番上に重ねた紙のみを自由に型抜き加工している。	グラフィックデザイン Graphic Design A graphic design studio established in 1992 by graphic designer, Masayuki Terashima, characterized by work that has a sense of fun as well as being beautifully designed. The company's business tools consist of business cards and envelopes. The back of the business card is the same for all staff members, but each designer has produced his or her own design for the side on which the name is printed, meaning each of the cards has a different typeface and layout. They have been made from three layers of cardstock with the top layer undergoing a die-cutting process.

Japan　AD, D: 寺島賢幸　Masayuki Terashima　D: 藤田直樹　Naoki Fujita / 佐藤建一　Kenichi Sato / 川本真也　Shinya Kawamoto / 森 雅代　Masayo Mori / 三平みどり　Midori Mihira / 郷古幸恵　Sachie Goko
DF, S: 寺島デザイン制作室　Terashima Design Co.

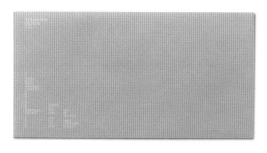
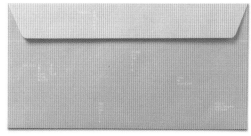

HAHMO

Hahmo Design Ltd.

フィンランドのデザインオフィスHahmo Design Ltd.は2003年に開業。グラフィックデザインをメインに、空間デザインから製品開発、コンセプト作りまでと幅広く活動する。オフィスのステーショナリーのすべてには黄色い枠が施され、枠の中身を強調するデザインとなっている。

Hahmo Design Ltd. is a Finland-based design agency founded in 2003, offering full range of services in graphic, spatial, product, and concept development. Office's stationeries are designed with a yellow frame to highlight the message within.

Finland   AD, D: Pekka Piippo / Antti Raudaskoski   D: Jenni Kuokka   DF, S: Hahmo Design Ltd.

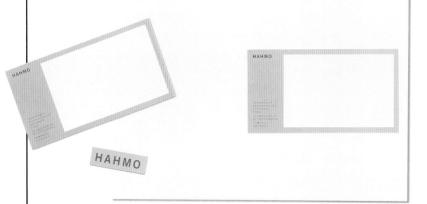

OUVI inc.

建築家・横尾 真が2005年に設立した、構造設計を中心としながら建築デザインまでも行う万能型建築事務所。自社ツール（名刺・封筒・DM）の作成は、「氏デザイン」が担当。ロゴデザインは、よく見ると「OUVI」の文字と判別できる色面で表現し、建築を影ながら支える構造設計の重要さを主張している。ツールにはロゴを大胆に使用し、特徴のある社名を前面に押し出している。

An all-round architectural design office established in 2005 by architect, Shin Yokoo, that offers architectural design with a focus on structural design. The company's tools (business cards, envelopes, DM) were produced by ujidesig. If you look closely at the design of the logo, you can make out the characters for OUVI shown with different color planes, demonstrating the idea of the importance of structural design in supporting a building. Bold use has been made of the logo on the business tools with the unusual company name very much at the forefront.

Japan   AD, DF, S: 氏デザイン ujidesign

移転案内 Moving Announcement

マック　MAQ inc.

広告企画制作
Creative Agency

MAQ inc.TOKYO

東京・大阪を拠点に、広告制作、グラフィックデザイン、ウェブなど、さまざまなフィールドで活動しているクリエイティブカンパニー。主に名刺や封筒など、アプリケーション用として活用しているロゴは、正式な社名ロゴ **MAQ** とは別に、東阪がパラレルなクリエイティブ会社であることをアピールするために開発されたもの。自社ツールは名刺と封筒。3種類のブランドポスターを、アプリケーションペーパーと位置付け、各ポスターから名刺一人あたり18種類、封筒30種類を制作している。印刷には特色2色＋蛍光オレンジ、ロゴのドットはシルク印刷を採用している。

A creative company with offices in Tokyo and Osaka that is active in various fields such as graphic design and the Web. The logo used on the business cards and envelopes was developed separately from the official company name logo for marketing the parallel creative company. The company's business tools are business cards and envelopes. The three types of brand poster were reserved as paper for their design applications, with business cards and envelopes were produced from each poster. They were printed in two match colors plus fluorescent orange, and the dots on the logo were silkscreen printed, demonstrating an attention to detail.

Japan　　CD: 山阪佳彦　Yoshihiko Yamasaka　　AD: 苧田健一　Kenichi Oda　　D: 角南貴雅　Takamasa Sunami / 柳田昌信　Akinobu Yanagida / 岸本敬子　Keiko Kishimoto　　P: 平田浩基　Hiromoto Hirata
DF, S: マック　MAQ inc.

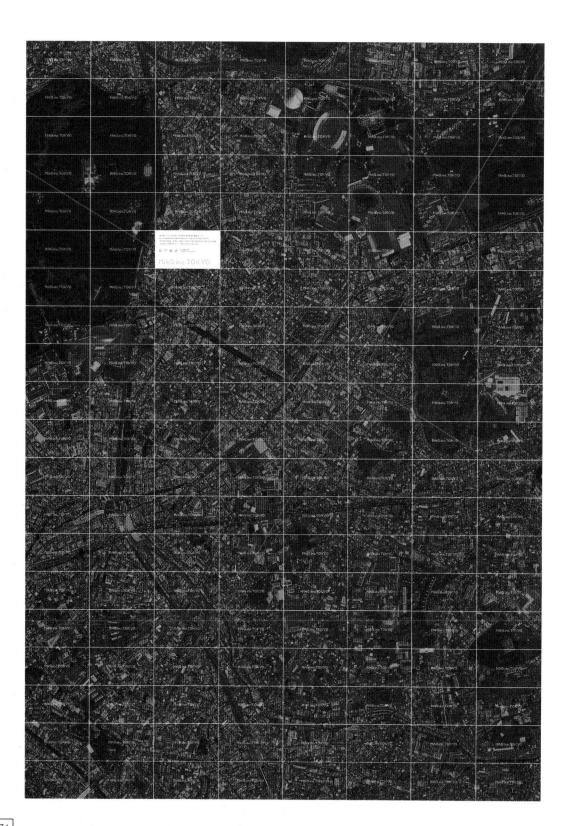

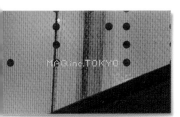

モーメント　MOMENT Inc.

グラフィック、プロダクト、インテリア、建築等、ジャンルを超えたデザインを提案するデザイン会社。3度の変更を重ねたロゴは、基本的に以前のロゴを踏襲しつつも、シンプルで安定感のある印象を持つようにリデザインされている。自社ツールは名刺、封筒、年賀状、移転案内。名刺はコーポレートカラーのブラック（実際にはCMYK、マットニス、グロスニスの6色印刷）を全面に押し出したデザインで、小口にもブラック印刷を施している。見る角度によって様々な黒が現れ、同社の持つ多様性を表現している。

A design company that offers design services across various genres. Moment's logo, which has been redesigned three times, basically follows the example of the previous logo with a simple, solid appearance. The company's business tools consist of business cards, envelopes, New Year cards and a change of premises notice. The surface of the business cards has been printed with the corporate color of black (actually they have printed with CMYK, matte varnish and gloss varnish) and small areas have been printed in black also. The various shades of black appear as you look at the card from different angles and express the diversity for which Moment is known.

Japan　　AD, D: 渡部智宏　Tomohiro Watabe / 平錦久晃　Hisaaki Hirawata　　DF, S: モーメント　MOMENT Inc.

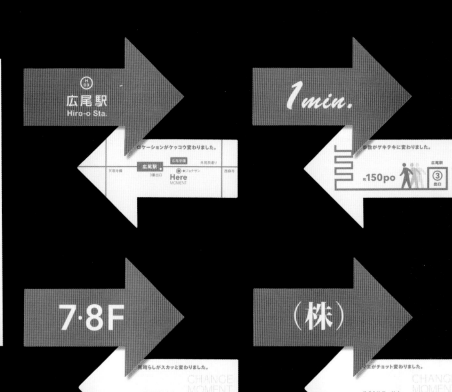

移転案内 Moving Announcement

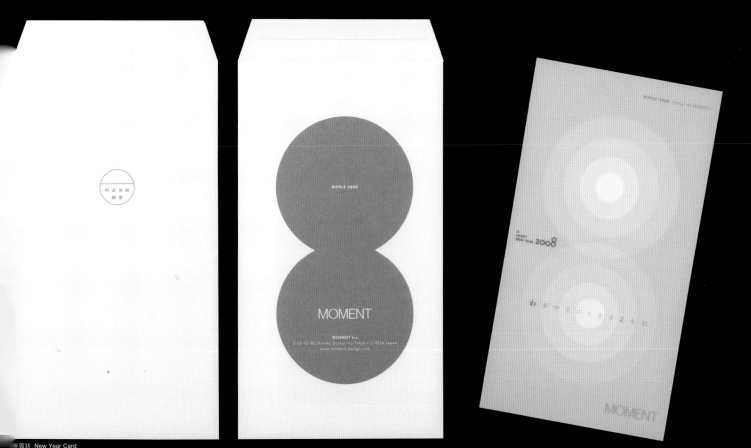

年賀状 New Year Card

サムライ　SAMURAI Inc.

クリエイティブスタジオ
Creative Studio

クリエイティブディレクター兼アートディレクターの佐藤可士和が代表をつとめ、広告、ロゴデザイン、商品パッケージから携帯電話などの工業デザイン、CIやブランディングまで、幅広い分野で活躍するクリエイティブスタジオ。社名の由来は、佐藤可士和の「士」の文字をとり「サムライ」と命名した。ロゴも社名同様に「士」の文字をデザイン化したものを採用。自社ツールは、名刺、封筒、レターヘッド、グリーティングカード等。全てのツールにシルバーの箔押し加工を施し、このシルバーをブランドカラーとしている。

A creative agency, represented by creative director and art director Kashiwa Sato, that has an extensive range of activity in the fields of advertising, logo design, product packaging, and industrial design of such things as the mobile phone, CI and branding. The company's name originated from the Japanese kanji character shi used in the name Kashiwa, a character that has a samurai connotation. The same character was also used for the logo. The company's range of business tools includes business cards, envelopes, letterhead and greeting cards and all have undergone a foiling process in silver, known as Samurai's brand color.

Japan　　CD, AD: 佐藤可士和 Kashiwa Sato　　D: 石川 耕 Ko Ishikawa / 江藤 源 Gen Eto / 奥瀬義樹 Yoshiki Okuse / 笠原智敦 Tomoatsu Kasahara　　DF, S: サムライ SAMURAI Inc.

ground

クリエイティブディレクター・高松 聡とアートディレクター・野尻大作を中心に2005年に設立されたクリエイティブエージェンシー。社名はオフィスを元中学校の建物内に構えていることから、「校庭」をイメージ して命名された。ロゴはgroundの「o」を、400メートルトラックをモチーフに制作した。封筒や 会社設立案内にはブルーグレーを使用し、清潔感を感じるデザインに。名刺は4色のカラーバリエーションがあり、名刺ボックスには名刺の渡し方がピクトグラムと英語で記載されている。

A creative agency set up in 2005 and headed up by creative director, Satoshi Takamatsu, and art director, Daisaku Nojiri. The company name contains the fact that the company is housed in what used to be a junior high school conjures up the image of "school grounds." The logo has taken the letter "o" in the word "ground" to produce a motif of a 400-meter track. The envelopes and the company profile have been produced in blue grey and have clean, intelligent look. The business cards come in four colors and the business card box uses pictograms to show ways of handing over a business card.

Japan   CD, AD: 野尻大作 Daisaku Nojiri   DF, S: ground

設立案内 Establishment Invitation

年賀状 New Year Card

年賀状 New Year Card

イー　E. Co., Ltd.

アートディレクター・蝦名龍郎を中心に、広告、グラフィックデザイン、CIやブランディングなど、幅広い分野で活躍するクリエイティブプロダクション。常によいものを作り続けたい、という社のコンセプト。ロゴはあえてシンプルで飽きのこないデザインに。自社ツールは、名刺、封筒、レターヘッド、ファイル等。封筒はサイズ別に色を変え、用途に合わせて使用している。名刺もそれぞれが好きな色を選び、カラーバリエーションのあるデザインとなっている。

A creative agency led by art director, Tatsuo Ebina, and active part in a range of fields such as advertising, free papers, CI and branding. To symbolize the company's concept of wanting to continue to create good things, the logo has a simple design that will stand the test of time. The company's business tools consist of business cards, envelopes, letterheads and files. The envelopes are in a different color depending on their size and are each used for a particular purpose. Everyone chooses their favorite color from a range of colors for their own business card.

Japan　AD, D: 蝦名龍郎 Tatsuo Ebina　DF, S: イー　E. Co., Ltd.

スープ・デザイン　SOUP DESIGN inc.

雑誌、書籍、設計、内装など、多方面で才能を発揮する尾原史和が率いるデザイン事務所。現在はグラフィック部門と建築部門に分かれて活動している。自社ツールは名刺、封筒、シールなど多数。名刺は7年以上同じフォーマットを使用しているが、その時の気分や使用する用途に合わせて使い分けたいという独自の考えから、会社のロゴはあえて作らず、その時々に応じて書体を選んでいる。年賀状や移転案内なども、感情を揺り動かすを考えとし、毎回一から作るため、同じものはひとつしてないという。

A design office led by Fumikazu Ohara with a multi-faceted capability for such things as magazine and book design, graphic design and interior design. It has many business tools including business cards, envelopes and stickers. The business cards have had the same format for more than seven years, but from the unique idea of adapting the cards to the mood at the time and the purpose for which they are being used, a logo was not produced and a typeface is chosen whenever required. For the New Year cards and the change of premises notice also, the concept was "to stir emotions," and as they are created anew each time, one is never like the other.

Japan　AD: 尾原史和　Fumikazu Ohara　DF, S: スープ・デザイン　SOUP DESIGN inc.

SOUP DESIGN inc.
OHARA FUMIKAZU
#B SENDAGAYA POST OFFICE BLDG.
1-23-7 SENDAGAYA SHIBUYA-KU TOKYO
JAPAN 151-0051
TEL 03-6802-7193　FAX 03-6802-7194
E-MAIL soupdesign@violin.ocn.ne.jp

移転案内　Moving Announcement

ステッカー　Sticker

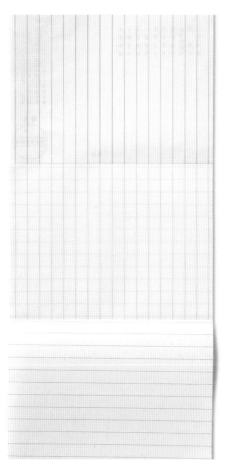

郵便はがき

料金別納郵便

年賀

株式会社メゾン・デザイン
東京都渋谷区神宮前六丁目二五番八号
神宮前コーポラス一〇三号室
電話　〇三-五七四四五六一三
ファクス〇三-五七四四五六一四

尾原　史和
川田　涼
阿部智佳子
中村　未里
塚原　敬史
未谷　知恵
漆原　慈一
岩間　良平
中島　破子
前田　亜希

謹賀新年
平素から格別のお引き立てをいただき
ありがとうございます。
これもひとえに皆様の多大なる
ご指導、ご鞭撻の賜物と感謝しております。
本年もスタッフみんなで
一層の精進をしていく所存でございます。
どうぞよろしくお願いいたします。
平成二〇年　元旦

追伸、
年が明けたあたに
気付いた方もいた事務
所の引っ越しをしまし
ておりますその節
にはますますの御
にはめて連絡を
差し上げますね尾

年賀状 New Year Card

xenön

ゼノン xenön

映画関係のポスターやパンフレット、企業や大学のカタログのデザインから広告の企画制作等を手がけるグラフィックデザイン事務所。会社の封筒や名刺は、長い間頻繁に使用するツールなので楽しくて、少しまじめで、飽きにくいものにしたいという想いを込め、郵便局、飛行場、役所などパブリックスペースにあるステッカーやパッケージのデザインを目標にして作成した。ステッカーは、封筒を閉じるテープとしても、切り離して差出人ツールとしても使用できるようになっている。

A graphic design office involved in a range of services from the design of film-related posters and pamphlets and catalogues to advertising planning and production. Because the company's envelopes and business cards will be in frequent use over a long period of time, the idea was that they be "fun but a little serious and something that people would not tire of easily," and it was decided they should look like the stickers and packaging commonly found in public places such as post offices, airports and government offices. The stickers serve as both a tape for sealing the envelopes shut and also as an address label.

Japan   AD, D: 岩波眞里 Mari Iwanami   DF, S: ゼノン xenön

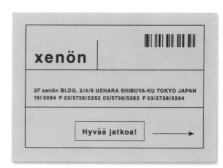

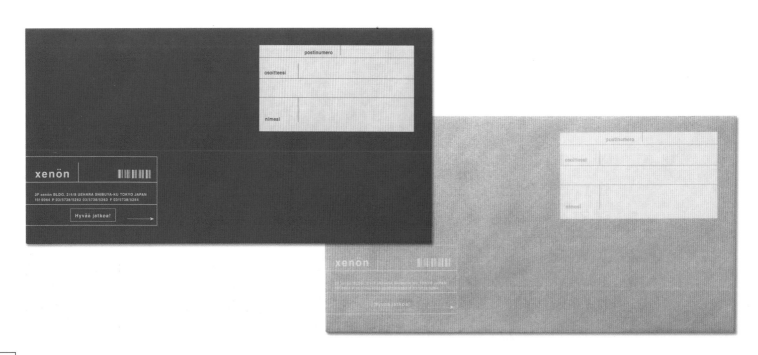

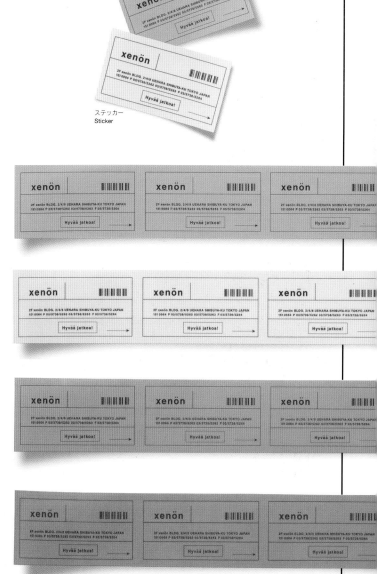

ステッカー
Sticker

TOKYO PISTOL CO., LTD.

東京ピストル　TOKYO PISTOL CO., LTD.

草彅洋平、加藤賢策、大西隆介、内川たくや、紙谷岳志の5人からなるデザイン会社。広告全般、大学関連、企業VI、雑誌、書籍、ウェブサイトなどのデザイン制作ならびに編集業務だけでなく、自主企画によるイベント運営、グッズ製作までを幅広く行っている。ロゴのコンセプトは、社名である「TOKYO PISTOL」の頭文字を組み合わせて、ピストルの形をシルエットで表現している。全ての自社ツールに同ロゴを採用し、黒1色刷りというストイックなデザインで統一している。

A design office headed by Yohei Kusanagi and four others (Kensaku Kato, Takasuke Onishi, Takuya Uchikawa and Takeshi Aratani) that provides an extensive range of design and editing services in relation to advertising, academic and corporate VI, magazines, books and websites, managing Tokyo Pistol special events and production of merchandise. The idea behind the logo is to turn the letter "T" in Tokyo and "P" in pistol into the shape of a pistol. The same logo has been used in all the company's business tools and unifies them with a stoic design in the one color of black.

Japan　CD: 草彅洋平　Yohei Kusanagi　AD: 加藤賢策　Kensaku Kato / 大西隆介　Takasuke Onishi　DF, S: 東京ピストル　TOKYO PISTOL CO., LTD.

バッジ　Badge

ステッカー　Sticker

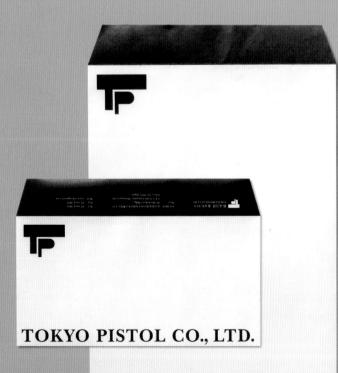

ノート Notebook

オリジナルグッズ Original Merchandise

Iro イロ Iro Co., Ltd.

デザイナー・干場邦一を中心に、オリジナル服飾ブランド「no quiet」のプレス、セールスの他、ブランド商品やノベルティのプロデュース、ブランド構築やスペースデザイン等、幅広い事業展開を行っているアパレルメーカー。また、グラフィックデザイン、インテリアデザイン、パッケージング等のデザイン制作全般の業務も行っている。自社ツールは名刺、封筒、ステッカー。名刺は紙の黒さにこだわり、スーパーコントラストのスーパーブラック160kgを使用し、四隅には角丸加工を施している。

An apparel manufacturer headed by the designer, Kunikazu Hoshiba, that has developed a diverse range of business interests including the production of brand products and novelties, brand building and space design, in addition to the press and sales for the original outfitting brand no quiet. Iro also provides a full complement of design production services that includes graphic design, interior design and packaging. Particular attention was given to the blackness of the card used for the business cards, and a super-contrast super black 160kg was used. The business cards then underwent a special process to have their corners rounded.

Japan   D: 干場邦一 Kunikazu Hoshiba   Product Section: 安田志穂 Shiho Yasuda   S: イロ Iro Co., Ltd.

ステッカー Sticker   DM

2-4-3 mita, meguro-ku, tokyo 153-0062
Tel 03-5773-1566 Fax 03-5773-1567
11:00-20:00 close on Wed.
www.noquiet.jp

● no quiet base shop

no quiet
no quiet
no quiet
no quiet
no quiet
no quiet
no quiet
no quiet
no quiet

kunikazu hoshiba

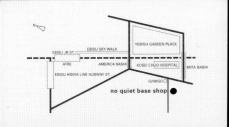

N

EBISU JR ST. | EBISU SKY WALK | YEBISU GARDEN PLACE

ATRE | AMERICA BASHI | KOSEI CHUO HOSPITAL | MITA BASHI

EBISU HIBIYA LINE SUBWAY ST.

GINKGO

no quiet base shop ●

ショップカード　Shop Card

てぬぐい　Towel

DM

no quiet
no quiet
no quiet
no quiet
no quiet
no quiet
no quiet

no quiet

no q

no quiet

no

kunikazu hoshiba

quiet

o quiet

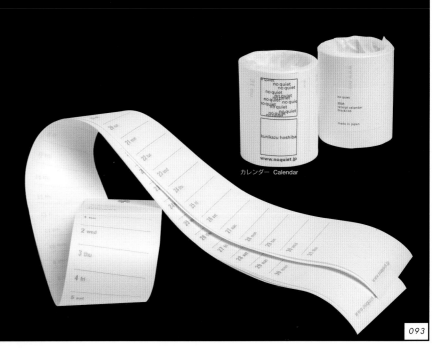

カレンダー　Calendar

SAFARI inc.

サファリ　SAFARI inc.

CI、VI、広告、パッケージ、エディトリアル等のグラフィックデザイン全般の制作をしているデザイン事務所。社名の「SAFARI」はアラビア語で「冒険」を意味する言葉。「いつまでも好奇心を大切に冒険していきたい」との想いが込められている。ロゴのコンセプトは、「デザイン的にあくまでニュートラルな状態でいたい」という社の方針から、あえてデザイン性を強く持たせないシンプルなものを採用。自社ツールは名刺、封筒、レターヘッド、年賀状など。名刺は、2枚並べると方位磁石の形になり、社名同様に「冒険」をイメージしたものとなっている。

A design office that provides the complete spectrum of graphic design services such as CI, VI, advertising, packaging and editorial. The word "safari" is the Arabic word for adventure, and encapsulates the idea of "being curious about the world and having a sense of adventure." Based on the company's policy of "in terms of design, maintaining a position that is always neutral," the concept for the logo is simple and the design is daringly understated. The company's business tools consist of business cards, envelopes, letterhead and New Year cards. Two of the business cards arranged side-by-side form a compass, conjuring up the idea of adventure.

Japan　　AD, D: 古川智基　Tomoki Furukawa　　AD: 荻田 純　Jun Ogita　　DF, S: サファリ　SAFARI inc.

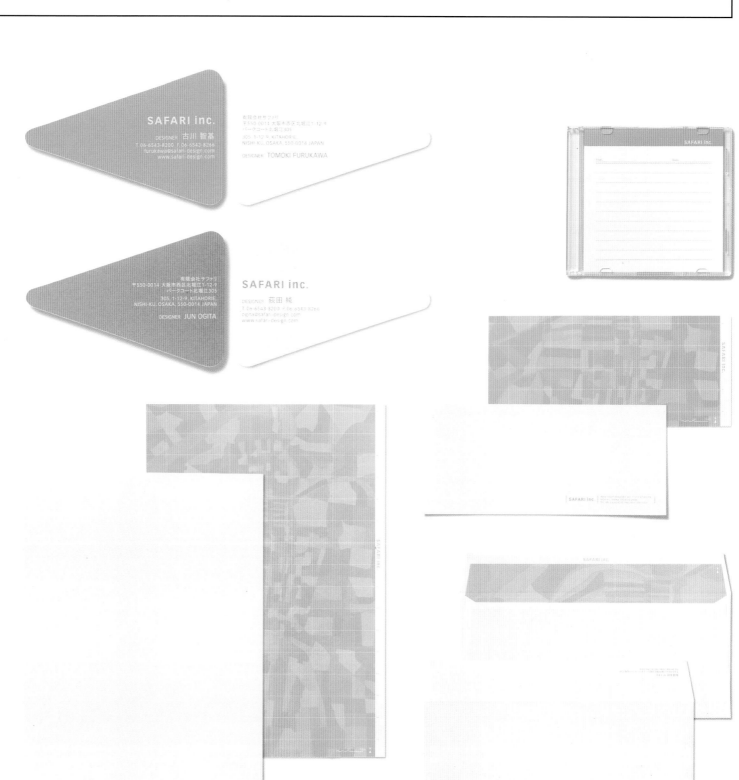

年賀状　New Year Card

移転案内　Moving Announcement

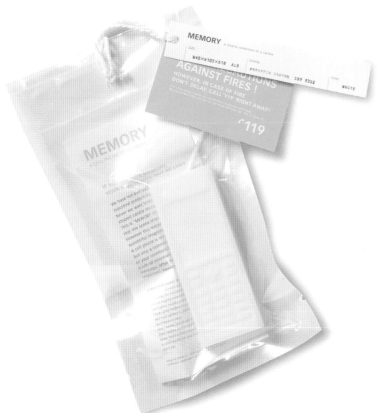

オリジナルグッズ　Original Merchandise

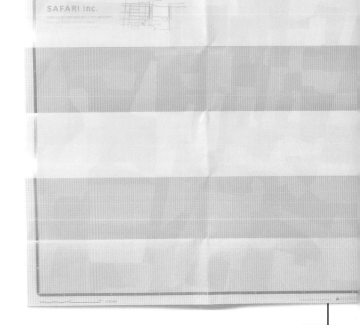

パラドックス・クリエイティブ　PARADOX CREATIVE INC.

広告やクリエイティブツールの企画制作を行うクリエイティブエージェンシー。新しい価値を創っていくことをコンセプトに掲げている同社は、新しいこととは、常識を疑うことから生まれるのでは、との考えから、「パラドックス」＝「逆説」という屋号とした。自社ツールは、名刺、封筒、ノベルティーとして制作しているカレンダー等。名刺や封筒等の基本ツールは、ブルーとシルバーグレーで統一、封筒には厚紙を使用しており、実用性を追求した。東京をはじめとして、大阪、名古屋、福岡にもオフィスを構え、それぞれのテーマに沿った、個性的な内装となっている。

Creative agency providing advertising and planning and production of creative tools. Paradox takes as its concept the idea of creating new value, and its name from the idea that new things arise out of questioning so-called common sense. Promotional tools include business cards, envelopes, novelty calendars etc. The basic tools such as business cards and envelopes are produced in a uniform blue and silver gray, with heavyweight paper employed for the envelopes with practicality in mind. The company has offices in Tokyo, Osaka, Nagoya and Fukuoka, each with a distinctly individual interior on a particular theme.

Japan　　DF, S: パラドックス・クリエイティブ PARADOX CREATIVE INC.

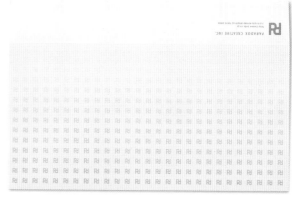

1. 大阪 Osaka, 2. 東京 Tokyo, 3. 福岡 Fukuoka, 4. 名古屋オフィス Nagoya Office

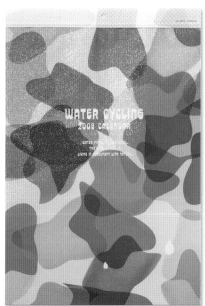

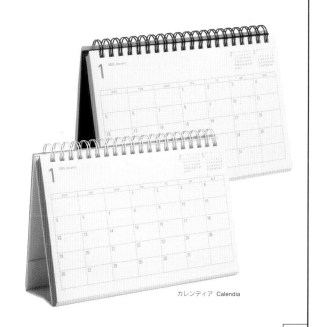

カレンダー Calendar

カレンディア Calendia

氏デザイン　ujidesign

2005年にアートディレクター・前田 豊により設立されたグラフィックデザイン事務所。グラフィック、広告、エディトリアル、VI、WEB、サイン、空間などのデザインを中心に活動中。社のコンセプトは「人を大切にするデザイン事務所」。ロゴデザインは、社名にもある通り、人の敬称に用いる「氏」という漢字をシンボルとして使用している。自社ツールは名刺、年賀状、DM等がある。

A graphic design office established in 2005 by graphic designer, Yutaka Maeda, that operates mainly in graphic design, advertising, editorial, VI, Web, signage and spaces. The company's concept is "a design office that values people." The logo design uses the kanji character for shi, an honorific title for a person, the same character that is used for the word uji in the company name. The company's business tools consist of business cards, New Year cards and DM.

Japan　AD, DF, S: 氏デザイン　ujidesign

a happy new year 2008　　　a happy new year 2008

年賀状　New Year Card

設立案内　Establishment Invitation

デザインルーム ウィルス　design room VIRUS

格好良さだけではなく、ぬくもり感を大切にデザインしているインテリアデザイン事務所。同社のロゴおよび自社ツールは、デザイン事務所の「SAFARI inc.」が手がけている。ロゴに使用されている横一直線のバーはVIRUS（ウィルス）ワールドの広がりを表現している。ツールは名刺、封筒、年賀状、移転案内。どの色にも染まらないイメージにしたかったため、モノクロをキーカラーに指定した。また温かみや味わいの出るよう紙選びにもこだわりを見せている。

An interior design office whose concept is design that is not only "cool" but also "warm." The design office SAFARI inc. was responsible for the company's logo and its business tools. The straight horizontal bar used for the logo expresses the expansion of the VIRUS world. The business tools include business cards, envelopes, New Year cards and a change of premises notice. Monochrome was chosen as the key color palette for a cool and stoic look. The selection of the paper, which is both warm and interesting also convey an attention to detail.

Japan　AD, D, P: 古川智基　Tomoki Furukawa　DF, S: サファリ　SAFARI inc.

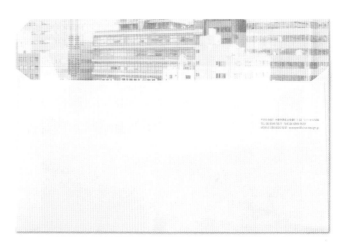

移転案内　Moving Announcement

エムディファクトリー　MD FACTORY INC.

MDFは、マーチャンダイジングファクトリーの略。商品開発、企画、製造など、クリエイティブに関することは平面から立体までトータルプロデュースしている。ロゴは、太くエッジを効かせたシンプルな字体の中に、仕事に対する誇りと力強さを込めてデザイン。名刺や封筒などの自社ツールのほかにノベルティーを制作し、年2回の季節の挨拶として送付している。手に取った人が驚くような、斬新なアイデアを盛り込んだ物を制作しており、発想から素材選び、デザインにいたるまで、常に「MDF」らしさを演出することを心がけている。

MDF is an abbreviation for "merchandising factory." MDF offers a comprehensive production service for both two- and three-dimensional design in the areas of product development and planning, and production. The logo has a heavy, edgy yet simple typeface that contains the company's pride in its the work and also its strength. In addition to the company's business tools, a range of novelties was produced which are sent out twice annually as season greetings. The items are based on novel ideas to delight the people who receive them and represent the essence of MDF, from the ideas to the selection of materials and the design.

Japan　CD, AD: イトーショータ Shohta Itoh　DF, S: エムディファクトリー　MD FACTORY INC.

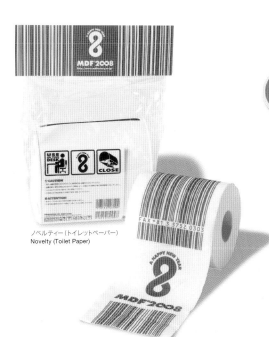

メモ帳 Memo Pad

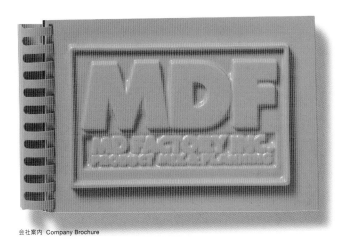

会社案内 Company Brochure

ノベルティー（トイレットペーパー）
Novelty (Toilet Paper)

移転案内 Moving Announcement

ノベルティー（製氷器） Novelty (Ice Tray)

TGB design.

石浦 克、小宮山秀明、市古斉史の3人により、1994年に結成されたデザインユニット。グラフィックデザインをはじめ、モーショングラフィックスやCM、PV、Web、インターフェイス、プロダクト、キャラクターデザイン制作など、その活動は多岐にわたる。また、企業ブランディング、商品企画などのトータルディレクションも手がけている。ロゴは、3DCGでありながら、柔らかさを感じるデザインに。金ののべ棒を紙で作ることをコンセプトにした箱には、TGBのエンブレムが箔押しされ、名刺と会社概要が中に同封されている。(www.tgbdesign.com)

A design unit formed in 1994 by Masaru Ishiura, Hideaki Komiyama and Masashi Ichifuru that is involved in a wide range of design activity from graphic design to motion graphics, CM, PV, Web, interface, product and character design and production. It also offers a comprehensive design service for corporate branding and product planning. Although the logo is 3DCG, a soft look has been achieved. On the boxes where the concept was creating a gold bar out of paper, the TGB emblem has undergone a foiling process and the business cards and company profile are then enclosed inside.

Japan   CD, AD, D, DF, S: TGB design.

封筒 Envelope

会社案内 Company Brochure

Webサイト戦略から表面設計、グラフィックデザイン、各種パブリッシングデザインまで、トータルに企画・運営する制作会社。自社ツール（名刺・封筒・レターヘッド・移転案内）の作成は、「氏デザイン」が担当。同社のロゴは、さまざまな用途に対応できるようにと、指定色を固定せずに自由な配色で使用し、自社ツールは、上記ロゴをタグに見立てて配置している。名刺は、それぞれのスタッフが自由に選んだ色でロゴが印刷されている。

A production company that offers comprehensive planning and management services from website strategy to surface design, graphic design and various kinds of publishing design. There was no designated color scheme established for the logo; instead optional color schemes were adopted so that the logo could be applied to various situations. The logo was likened to a tag to be placed on the company's business tools. The logo is printed on the business cards in colors chosen by individual staff members.

Japan　AD, DF, S: 氏デザイン　ujidesign

ギークピクチュアズ　GEEK PICTURES INC.

CM制作プロダクション
Commercial Production Company

TV、Webコマーシャルの企画・制作から、エンターテイメントコンテンツの企画・制作・販売、映像に関連するプロモーション、キャラクターの企画・開発、クリエイターのマネジメント業務などを行っているCM制作プロダクション。ロゴおよび自社ツールはシンガタが手がけている。ロゴのデザインは、「映像のオタクでありたい」という社の意志をふまえ、モニターをイメージさせる枠を2点組み合わせて頭文字の「g」を表現した。自社ツールは名刺と封筒。シンプルな白封筒にスミでロゴを印刷、宛名を書くスペースをエンボス加工で表している。

A commercial production company involved in a range of activity from planning and production of TV and Web commercials, planning, production and sale of entertainment content, audiovisual-related promotion, development of characters and management of creators. Shingata Inc. was responsible for the design of the logo and the company's business tools. Based on the company's desire to be regarded as "the geek of the audiovisual world," two frames that resemble a monitor have been to express the letter "g" in the word "geek." The logo is printed on simple white envelopes in black and the space for writing the address has undergone an embossing process.

Japan　AD: 水口克夫 Katsuo Mizuguchi　D: 久松陽一 Youichi Hisamatsu / 山中牧子 Makiko Yamanaka　DF: シンガタ Shingata Inc.　S: ギークピクチュアズ GEEK PICTURES INC.

エイチーズ　H's

広告制作会社
Advertising Agency

コピーライティングを中心とした広告制作会社。ロゴおよび自社ツールのデザインは、アートディレクター・永田武史らが所属している広告制作会社「イー」が手がけている。ロゴデザインのコンセプトは、コピーライティングを中心とした会社らしく、「H's」のアポストロフィーの部分が、マンガの「フキダシ」の形にデザインされている。自社ツールは、名刺、封筒、レターヘッド、紙袋、スタンプ。どのツールも「気づいた人が「ハッ!」として、そこからコミュニケーションが生まれるように」をコンセプトに制作されている。

An advertising production company that deals mainly in copywriting. The advertising production company E. Co., Ltd. to which art director Takeshi Nagata belongs, was responsible for the design of the logo and the company's business tools. The concept for the logo involves making the apostrophe in H's into the kind of speech bubble seen in comics – a fitting design for a company devoted mainly to copywriting. The company's business tools include business cards, envelopes, letterhead, paper bags and stamps. All the tools have been produced with the idea making the person who sees them go Wow! and thereby stimulating communication.

Japan　AD: 永田武史 Takeshi Nagata　D: 廣瀬 豊 Yutaka Hirose　DF, S: イー E. Co., Ltd.

CluB_A

葵プロモーションから独立したCMディレクターによるマネージメントオフィス。自社ツールおよびロゴは、アートディレクター・佐野研二郎が代表をつとめるデザインオフィス「MR_DESIGN」が担当。ロゴデザインのコンセプトは、「シンプルに誠実に」。シンプルな書体であるDINをベースに構成し、ネーミングにA、B、Cの文字を入れて強調した。自社ツールは、名刺、封筒、ステッカー。「A」を強調したタイポグラフィで、ロゴマニュアルやアドレスのリピートなど、シンプルで印象深いデザインとなっている。

A management office belonging to a director of television commercials. The design office MR_DESIGN represented by art director, Kenjiro Sano, was responsible for the design of the company's business tools and the logo. The concept for design of the logo was "simple and sincere." Constructed on a base of the simple font called DIN, the letters A, B and C were made part of the name for emphasis. The company's business tools are business cards, envelopes and stickers. With a typography that emphasizes the letter A, a simple yet memorable design has been produced by repetition of the logo manual and the address.

Japan   AD: 佐野研二郎 Kenjiro Sano   D: 遠藤祐子 Yuko Endo   DF, S: MR_DESIGN

ステッカー Sticker

Business to Arts

美術組織
Art Organization

アイルランドに所在するBusiness to Artsは企業とアーティストのパートナーシップ
を推進する団体。ロゴはこのコラボレーションを表現するためにArtの「A」と
Businessの「B」を融合させたユニークな形となっている。

Business to Arts is an Ireland based organization that facilitates partnerships between business and artists. Logo is designed to describe this collaborative nature of work, where 'A' of Arts and the 'B' of Business is united into a unique shape and recognizable form.

Ireland   D: Billy Kiossoglou / Frank Philippin   DF, S: Brighten the Corners

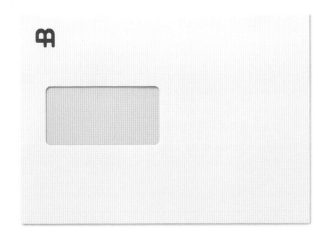

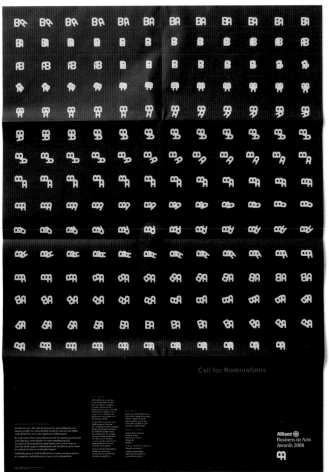

ポスター Poster

嶋岡 隆　TAKASHI SHIMAOKA

映画、テレビドラマ、雑誌等、幅広い分野で活躍しているスタイリスト。ツールのアートディレクションは、1960年設立の広告制作会社「たき工房」の木村高典によるもの。制作した嶋岡氏のツールは名刺、封筒、レターヘッド、シール、ブックカバー等。ロゴはスタイリストという職業を単純明快に示している。同氏のコンセプトが「ニュートラルでいること」であるのに対し、ツールのコンセプトは「ニュートラルではない見え方」を意識している。

A stylist whose extensive scope of activity includes films, TV dramas and magazines. The art direction for his business tools was undertaken by art director, Takanori Kimura, of the advertising production company, Taki Corporation that was set up in 1960. The range of Takashi Shimaoka's business tools includes business cards, envelopes, letterhead, stickers and book covers. The logo shows what a stylist is in a clear and simple way. In contrast to Takashi Shimaoka's own concept of "being neutral," the concept for his business tools contains an awareness of "appearing not to be neutral."

Japan　AD, D: 木村高典（たき工房）Takanori Kimura (TAKI CORPORATION)　D: 梅田将明（たき工房）Masaaki Umeda (TAKI CORPORATION)　DF, S: たき工房 TAKI CORPORATION

名刺入れ Card Case

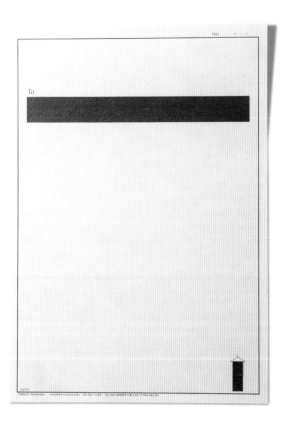

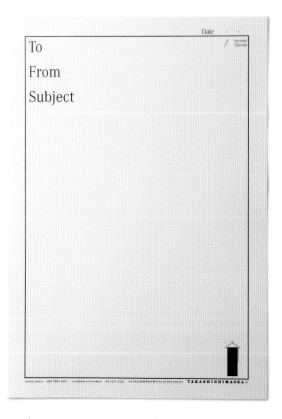

ブックカバー Book Jacket

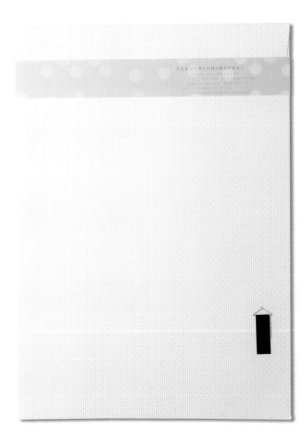
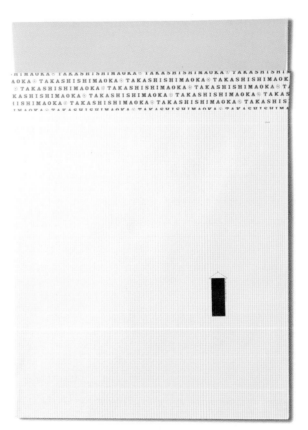

Nosigner

デザインの語源は、形に記す（de-sign）という意味。しかし優れたデザインは、自然界のもののように形のない、目に見えない必然から生まれるのでは、という考えと、あえてデザインをした者の名前は必要ないのでは、という想いから「見えないものをデザインする者」そして「名を名乗らない者」という意味を込めて「Nosigner」として活動している。名刺は、白い面に折り目が入っており、曲げると立体となる仕組みに。封筒は木漏れ日をイメージし、半透明の紙に白インキで木の葉を印刷している。用途や季節により、中に色紙を入れて使用している。

The origin of the word "design" is the description of something using forms (de-sign). However, from the belief that outstanding design emerges from a necessity that unlike the natural world has no form, and the idea that it is not necessary to know the name of the person who produced the design, the company works under the name "Nosigner". The white surface of the business cards contains crease lines which when folded make the cards three-dimensional. The envelopes evoke the idea of sunshine filtering through foliage with the leaves printed on semitransparent paper in white ink.

Japan   AD, D, S: Nosigner

MARVIN

マーヴィン　MARVIN

クリエイティブディレクター・Joan McCullochとアートディレクター・山本ヒロキを中心とした、広告、パッケージ、CI、イラストレーション、ブックデザイン等、グラフィック全般の分野で活躍しているデザイン事務所。ロゴはオリジナルフォントの「MARVIN BOLD」を使用。「A」の傾斜は「未来の向こう側へ傾けること」という、先鋭的デザインをしていく覚悟を表現している。自社ツールは名刺、封筒、グリーティングカード等。カードにはUVシルク印刷、型抜き、クニメタルなどの特殊加工・特殊用紙を用いている。

A design office headed by creative director, Joan McCulloch, and art director, Hiroki Yamamoto, that offers a comprehensive range of graphic design services including packaging, CI, illustration and book design. The logo uses Marvin's own typeface, Marvin Bold. The slant of the letter "A" expresses a readiness to create radical design, that is, "to lean beyond the future". The company's business tools include business cards, envelopes and greeting cards. The cards have undergone special UV silkscreen printing, die cutting and Kuny metal processes.

Japan　CD: ジョアン・マカロック　Joan McCulloch　　AD: 山本ヒロキ　Hiroki Yamamoto　　DF, S: マーヴィン　MARVIN

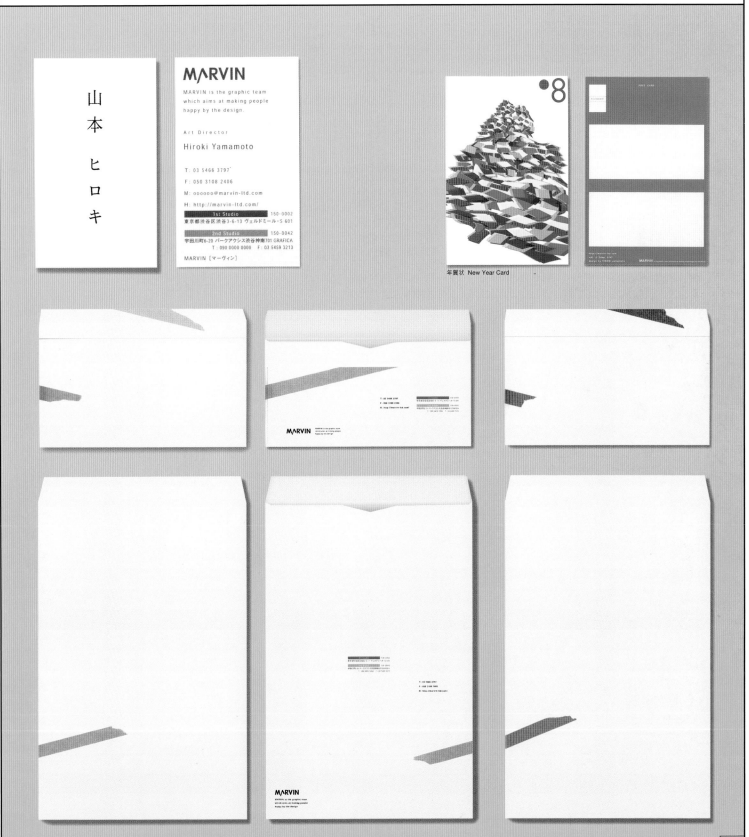

年賀状　New Year Card

Dominique Vézina

Dominique Vézina はロンドンで活躍するファッション・プロダクトデザイナー。細くしたHelveticaフォントに飾り文字を用いたロゴデザインと、洗練された中にも遊び心を融合させたオフィスステーショナリーはDominique Vézinaのスタイルをよく表している。

Dominique Vézina is a fashion and product designer based in London. Logo designed with the thin cut of Helvetica in combination with the ornamental pictograms represents her style well. Dominique's office stationeries are designed with straight and elegant nature combined with playfulness like her work.

UK   D: Billy Kiossoglou / Frank Philippin   DF, S: Brighten the Corners

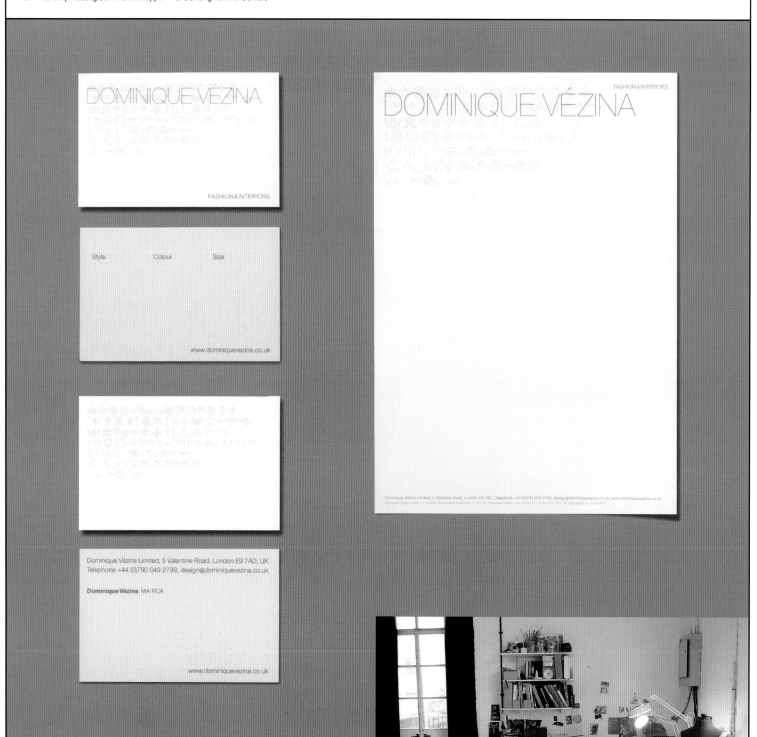

SMITHSPENCE

イギリスに所在するSMITHSPENCEはオート・クチュールをデザインするファッションハウス。現代にクラッシックな要素を取り入れているクチュールのスタイルはオフィスステーショナリーのデザインにも反映されている。ロゴにはクチュールが影響を受けた19世紀の書体を使用。完成商品のすべてに手書きで署名と番号をふるSMITHSPENCEでは名刺も署名や個人情報が記入できるデザインとなっている。

SMITHSPENCE is fashion house designs couture dresses, based in UK. The designs are directional but with a nod to classic, which also comes across in all the office stationeries. Its logotype adapts a classis typeface designed in the 1900's, which is an era of inspiration to the couture. As each garment is numbered and signed in completion, the business card is also designed to be hand written or signed by individuals.

UK   CD, D: Emma Thomas / Kirsty Carter   D: Stephen Osman   DF, S: A Practice for Everyday Life

カード Card

黒田 潔　Kiyoshi Kuroda

イラストレーター
Illustrator

イラストレーター、アートディレクターとして広告や雑誌のアートワークを手がけるとともに、海外での展示にも多数参加している。自社ツールは、名刺、封筒、ステッカー、DM等。名刺は、電通の佐藤俊一がオリジナルフォントから制作した。封筒は1点ずつシルクスクリーンで手刷りされており、柄がそれぞれ少しずつ異なる。ポストカードには、ゼブラの絵柄部分にUV加工が施されている。自身の作品を用いることで、印象的な自社ツールとなっている。

Kiyoshi Kuroda is an illustrator and art director who works in advertising and magazine production and participates in a large number of overseas exhibitions. His business tools include business cards, envelopes, sticker and DM. Shunichi Sato of Dentsu produced the business cards using an original font. The envelopes were each hand-printed separately with silkscreen, making the pattern slightly different on each. The illustration of the zebra on the postcards undergoing a UV process. An impressive set of business tools has resulted from the use of Kuroda's own artwork.

Japan　AD, D, I, S: 黒田 潔　Kiyoshi Kuroda　AD, D (a): 佐藤俊一（電通）　Shunichi Sato (DENTSU INC.)

ステッカー　Sticker

ポストカード　Post Card

DM

rubecksen yamanaka

rubecksen yamanakaはイギリスに所在するファッションハウス。素材の特性と色彩を楽しんで作られる洋服は繊細で美しい。オフィスステーショナリーにも同様のスタイルを取り入れ、特殊な印刷方法で独特な色彩と質感を紙に与えた繊細なデザインとなっている。

rubecksen yamanaka is a fashion house based in UK. Finely detailed and beautifully peculiar, they play with garment's changing characteristics and palette. Office stationeries reflect the feeling of these garments using thermo graphically printing technique to give fineness and interesting texture to the paper.

· rubecksen yamanaka ·

UK   CD, D: Kirsty Carter / Emma Thomas   DF, S: A Practice for Everyday Life

カタログ Catalogue

カード Card

Olivia Morris

Olivia Morrisはイギリスに所在する靴のデザイナーズブランド。ロゴは都会的で飽きさせないデザインに、オフィスステーショナリーにはブランドカラーであるグレーとゴールドを使用。2007年版のカタログとインビテーションには1950年代のハワイアンポスターに影響されたイラストを用いている。

Olivia Morris is a designer shoes brand based in England. The brand logo is designed to be personal, sophisticated and timeless. Office stationeries use her brand colors grey and gold. 2007 brochure and invitation use illustration inspired by 1950's Hawaiian posters.

UK   CD, AD, D, DF, S: STUDIOTHOMSON   P: Xanthe Greenhill   Logo Design: Alex Geoffrey

カタログ Catalogue

インビテーション Invitation

F1 メディア　F1 MEDIA inc.

F1層（20〜34歳の女性層）をターゲットにした、モバイル、WEB、イベント等を手がける媒体社。ロゴおよび自社ツールのデザインは博報堂のアートディレクター・長嶋りかこが担当。ステンシル調のロゴは、街の媒体が段々と同社にジャックされていく様を、スプレーのマーキングを使ったデザインで表現している。自社ツールは名刺、封筒、ポスター、ステッカー。ポスターは、ロゴマークのハートを使い、同社の仕掛けにより、女性たちの心が動かされている様を表現した。ステッカーは写真に貼ることによってポスターと同様の表現が可能となっている。

A media company that deals in mobile, Web, events etc targeted at the "F1 class" (females between 20 and 34 years old). Art director, Rikako Nagashima of Hakuhodo Co. Ltd. was responsible for the design of the logo and the company's business tools. The stencil-like logo expresses, using a spray effect, the gradual taking over of the city's media by F1 MEDIA inc. The company's business tools consist of business cards, envelopes, a poster and stickers. The poster uses the heart logo mark and expresses the idea of the company's gimmick capturing women's hearts. The same result as the poster is achieved when the stickers are placed on photographs.

Japan　CD: 笠井修二 Shuji Kasai　AD, D, S: 長嶋りかこ Rikako Nagashima　CW: 大八木 翼 Tsubasa Ooyagi　P: 青山たかかず Takakazu Aoyama　D, I: 水溜友絵 Tomoe Mizutamari
Producer: 星本和容 Kazuhiro Hoshimoto　DF: シロップ Syrup inc.

ステッカー　Sticker

ポスター　Poster

ポスター　Poster

Reptile's House

Reptile's Houseはイタリアに所在するファッションブランド。通常とは異なるデザインにするため、名刺には大きく軽い紙を使用、簡単に折り曲げられて裏面はメモ用紙として使える。インビテーションカードは、ブランドの商品写真に多数の穴を開けて加工されたエレガントでオリジナリティのあるデザイン。もう一つのインビテーションカードは、商品イラストと写真を自由に組み合わせられる冊子がボール紙に輪ゴムで縛り付けられている。

Reptile's House is a fashion brand based in Italy. Business card is designed to not become the typical business card, by preferring a large and a light paper, easy to fold and can be used for notes on the back. On its show invitation, photo of a bag from the collection is used with multiple small holes punched for an original and elegant look. Another invite is made cutting and mixing photo of collection's products and their original illustration: the two pamphlets are joined to a thick cardboard with a rubber band.

Italy   CD: Marco Molteni / Margherita Monguzzi   I: alvvino.org   DF, S: jekyll & hyde

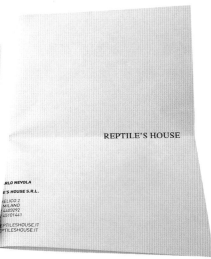

DM

DM

THREEASFOUR

ファッションデザイン
Fashion Design

THREEASFOURはニューヨークに所在するファッションデザイン事務所。ファッションショーのインビテーションとカタログは各コレクションの特徴を表したデザインになっている。洋服のラベルやタグには太い輪ゴムを使用。THREEASFOURのコレクションをまとめた8冊の冊子は、表紙にロゴが箔押しされた特注の布製本箱に収まっており、1冊に1つのコレクションが紹介されている。スクリーン印刷された冊子は重ねて置くとロゴが表れる作りとなっている。

THREEASFOUR is a fashion design office based in NYC. Fashion show invites and look books are inspired by each collection. For labels and tags, modular system of rubber bands are used. THREEASFOUR book created in a series of 8 booklets is enclosed in a specially made linen covered box that was foil stamped with their logo. Each booklet represents one of their collections. The covers are screen printed so that when all of the books are seen together they form the logo.

USA   CD, AD, D, DF, S: STILETTO NYC

ポスター Poster

冊子 Booklet

Martyn Bal

Martyn Balは高級メンズファッションブランド。ロゴはMaxi Billが50年前にデザインした古い書体を使用、オリジナルの数学的で直線的なフォントをもとにMartyn Balブランドらしさを反映したフォルムへ加工している。オフィスステーショナリーには、ロゴと共にキュビズムの白鳥アイコンとCourier書体が、光沢のあるオフセットプリントでコーティング無しの紙に印刷されている。

Martyn Bal is a luxury menswear fashion brand. Logotype is based on a 50-year old letter type created by Max Bill. The original font represents rigor and mathematical complexity of the form, which was adopted as a shell for the MARTYN BAL identity and reworked to make it relevant to label's values. On office stationeries, logo is accompanied with the cubist icon of the swan and Courier font, which are offset printed with high gloss against uncoated paper.

Netherlands   D, S: Kasia Korczak   D: Boy Vereecken   Typographical Detail: Jeremy Johnson   Drawing: Karl Nawrot

カード Card   封筒 Envelope

ファイル File

NAOKI TAKIZAWA DESIGN

前ISSEY MIYAKEクリエイティブディレクターの滝沢直己が2007年7月に設立したファッションデザイン事務所。ブランドのコレクション以外でも、佐藤可士和、森山大道、村上 隆など、ファッションの枠組みを超えた多岐に渡る分野のクリエイター、アーティストとのコラボレーションを行っている。同社ロゴならびに自社ツールは、佐藤可士和のサムライが手がけた。ロゴデザインは、滝沢直己のイニシャルNとTをシンボル化したもの。自社ツールは名刺、封筒、レターヘッドで、ハイブランドならではのクオリティの高さを表現している。

A fashion design office set up in July 2007 by Naoki Takizawa who previously worked as creative director for Issey Miyake. In addition to creating the brand's collections, the company collaborates with creators and artists the likes of Kashiwa Sato, Daido Moriyama and Takashi Murakami, among others, in a diverse range of fields that transcend the world of fashion. The company's logo and its business tools were produced by Kashiwa Sato's Samurai firm. The logo design features the N and the T of Naoki Takizawa. The high quality of the company's business tools – the business cards, envelopes and letterhead - is what one would expect to see from such a high-quality brand.

Japan   CD, AD: 佐藤可士和 Kashiwa Sato   D: 江藤 源 Gen Eto   DF, S: サムライ SAMURAI Inc.

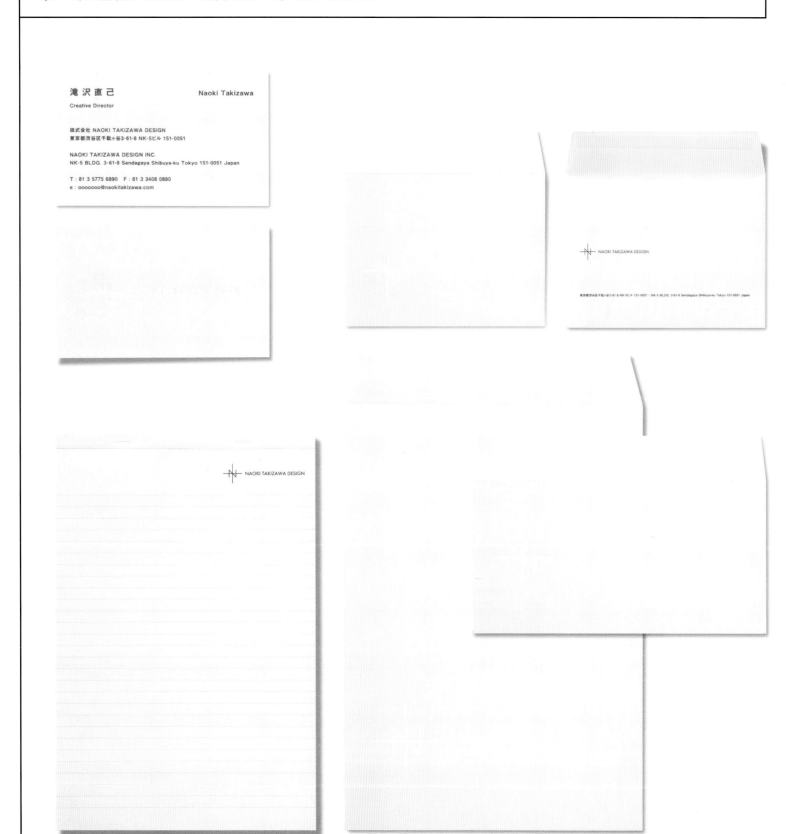

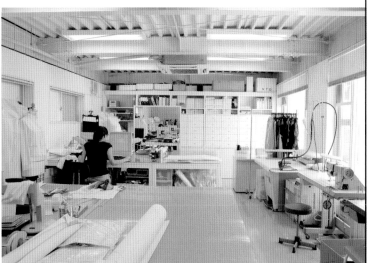

A Practice for Everyday Life

APFEL
A Practice for Everyday Life

ロンドンに所在するA Practice for Everyday Life[略:APFEL]はグラフィックデザインスタジオ。ロゴを黄色でハイライトすることによってスタジオ名の頭字語であることを強調。ノート用紙と便箋の裏側にはスタジオのフロアの模様を用いている。ノート用紙は、手紙やメモ用として使いやすく上品なA5サイズにしている。

A Practice for Everyday Life (APFEL) is a graphic design studio based in London. Logo uses archival method of a yellow highlight to draw attention to the acronym 'APFEL'. Pattern on the reverse side of the notepaper and the letterhead derives from APFEL's studio-flooring pattern. The notepaper is created in A5 size for its elegant and useful size to write notes and short letters.

UK   DF, S: A Practice for Everyday Life

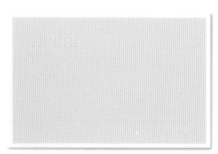

ステッカー Sticker

ノート用紙 Notepaper

樋口兼一写真事務所　KENICHI HIGUCHI PHOTO OFFICE

フォトグラファー
Photographer

広告や雑誌等で活躍する写真家・樋口兼一が設立した写真事務所。自社ツールのデザインはアートディレクター・山田信男（セントラルパーク）が担当した。ツールの種類は名刺、封筒、事務所移転案内、年賀状、4×5フィルムサイズBOX等。すべてのツールは高白色で上質な紙に黒一色で印刷し、統一されたブランドイメージを築いている。納品ツールは「自分にとって納品する写真は大切な作品。写真の保護は勿論、受け取った方が快く写真を使用できるように」という依頼を受け、上質で洗練されたデザインに仕上げている。

A photographic office established by photographer, Kenichi Higuchi who works in the production of CD inserts and magazines. The design office, Central Park, set up by art director, Nobuo Yamada, produced the company's business tools (business cards, envelopes, letterhead, change of premises notice, 4x5 film boxes). The words of the photographer himself were, "For me, the photos I produce for my clients are valuable works of art. I want the photos to be protected but I also want my clients to be able to enjoy them." The finished design is therefore elegant and refined.

Japan　AD, D: 山田信男　Nobuo Yamada　DF, S: セントラルパーク　CENTRAL PARK

ヴイキュー　VQ

フォトグラファー
Photographer

金子親一、田中良知、横山雅人、小柳 宏、田口陽介の5名が2006年に共同で立ち上げた写真事務所。自社ツールは、10（テン）のアートディレクター・柿木原政広が制作。名刺や封筒は動きのあるデザインを意識し、重たい書体を使用することで、受け取る人に強い印象を与えている。

A photographic office jointly set up in 2006 by Shinichi Kaneko, Yoshitomo Tanaka, Masato Yokoyama, Hiroshi Koyanagi and Yosuke Taguchi. The company's business tools were produced by the art director of 10, Masahiro Kakinokihara. The business cards and envelopes have a dynamic design and the heavy typeface gives their recipients an impression of strength.

Japan　AD, D: 柿木原政広 Masahiro Kakinokihara　DF, S: 10 Ten

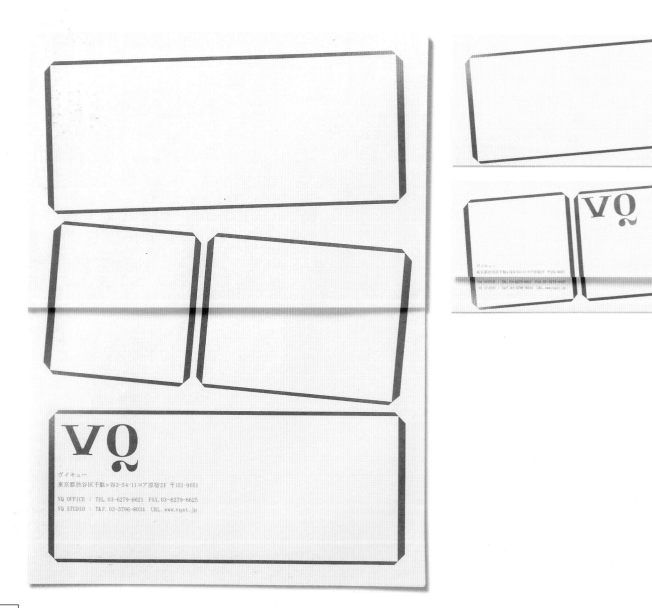

スナッピンブッダ　Snappin' Buddha

Snappin' Buddha

フォトグラファー・M. HASUIを中心に、8名のスタッフで運営する映像クリエイティブ会社。スティールだけではなく、コマーシャルフィルムの撮影や演出も手がけている。名刺・封筒などの自社ツールは、10（テン）のアートディレクター・柿木原政広が制作。グレーと白を基調とした清潔感のある色合いを使用し、潔いデザインとなっている。封筒は、プリントを納品する際にも使用するため強度を重視し、厚紙を使用している。

An audio-visual creative company run by M. Hasui and eight staff members. The company is involved in not only still photography but also the filming and production of commercial films. The company's business tools (business cards and envelopes) were produced by the art director of 10, Masahiro Kakinokihara. The clean colors of grey and white have been used to produce a pure design. The envelopes are made from cardboard for additional strength when proofs are delivered to customers.

Japan　　AD, D: 柿木原政広 Masahiro Kakinokihara　　DF, S: 10　Ten

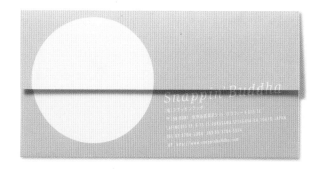

ウォールアンドリッタイ　WALL & LITTAI corporation

フォトグラファー
Photographer

2001年にフォトグラファー・泊昭雄がスタイリスト数名と共に立ち上げたギャラリー「WALL」が、写真家として、またクリエイターとしての発進のホームグラウンドになったことを受け、「立体」から現在の社名に変更。ロゴおよび自社ツール(名刺・封筒)は、アートディレクター・副田高行が設立した副田デザイン制作所が担当。ロゴデザインは、あえてオリジナルの文字を作成せず、シンプルで美しい丸明オールドの「泊」という漢字一文字を採用している。ツールの印刷もグレー1色のモノトーンで、きわめてシンプルなデザインとなっている。

The gallery WALL was set up in 2001 by photographer Akio Tomari together with several stylists. The gallery became his base both as a photographer and as a creator and his company name was subsequently changed from Littai to Wall & Littai. Soeda Design Factory (art director, Takayuki Soeda), was responsible for designing the logo and the company's business tools (business cards, envelopes). Characters were not specifically produced for the logo design. Instead, the single kanji character "tomari" in the Marumin Old typeface was used for the logo. The tools were printed in various shades of the single color of gray resulting in an extremely simple design.

Japan　AD: 副田高行 Takayuki Soeda　D: 貝塚智子 Tomoko Kaizuka　DF: 副田デザイン制作所 soeda design factory　S: ウォールアンドリッタイ WALL & LITTAI corporation

DM

Seed Media Group.

Seed Media Group.は科学の本、雑誌そして映像を手掛ける出版社。科学とメディアをビジュアル化するために、ロゴデザインには「葉序」の形が用いられている。葉序とは茎上の葉の配列であり、その構造は貝殻やギリシャ建築、パイナップルの形からシドニーのオペラハウス建築等々様々な所で見られる。置かれた環境に順応する「葉序」の形を活かし、名刺のロゴでは本人の肖像が浮き出すデザインに。便箋では玉虫色の光沢がその場所を映し出すなど工夫を凝らしている。

Seed Media Group is a scientific publisher of magazines, books and films. In order to visualize science and media in the logo, its design is based on the shape of 'phyllotaxis', a form found everywhere from Seashells to Greek architecture, from pineapples to the Sydney opera house. As the shape can take many forms depending on the media it is put on, on business card it shows a version of the portrait of the bearer, on he letterhead it iridescently reflects the room, etc.

USA   AD: Stefan Sagmeister   D: Matthias Ernstberger   DF,S: Sagmeister Inc.

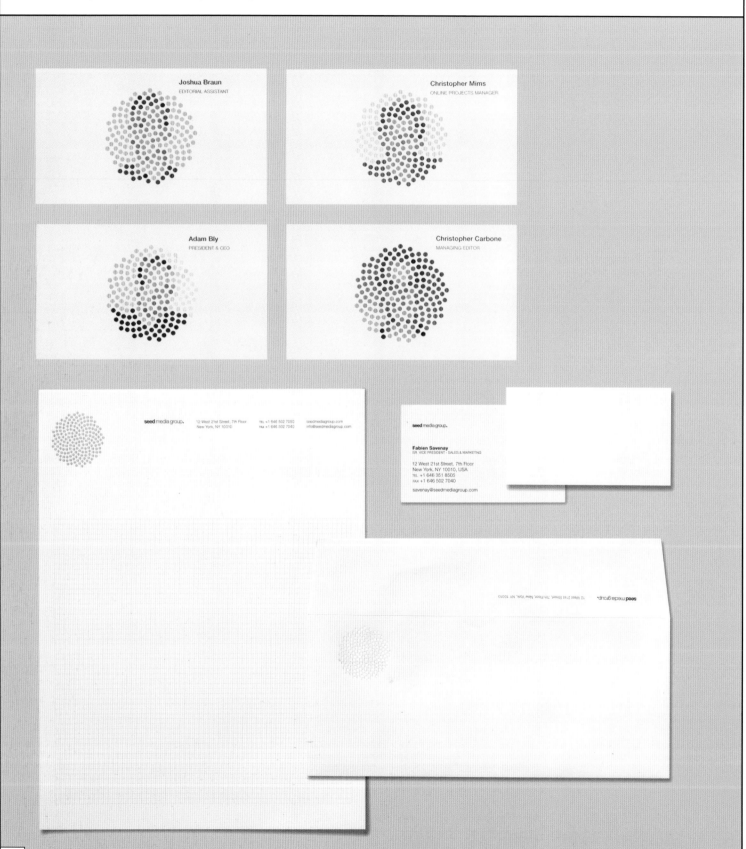

シブヤパブリッシング＆ブックセラーズ　SHIBUYA PUBLISHING & BOOKSELLERS, LLC

ブックショップと編集スペースが隣接し、編集者のミーティングスペースや編集スペースが店舗に面した通りからも書店側からも視認できる、「そこで作ってそこで売る」をコンセプトにした出版社。会社および店舗で使われるロゴのデザインは本棚のイメージをデザイン化したもの。自社ツールはcoldwater graphiixが手掛け、名刺、封筒、梱包材、ショッピングバッグなどがある。ロゴの棚の中央部分は、色によって法人名使用時（赤）、出版物使用時（青）、書店内備品使用時（黄）を使い分けている。

A publishing company consisting of a bookshop and an editorial space adjacent to each other. The editors' meeting space and the editorial space can be seen both from the street on which the shop stands and also from within the shop itself. Its concept is "produce here, sell here." The design of the logo used for both the corporate and retail divisions of the business incorporates a design of a bookshelf. The center shelf in the logo has a different color for each division of the company: red for Shibuya Publishing & Booksellers, blue for Shibuya Publishing and yellow for Shibuya Booksellers.

Japan　D: コールドウォーターグラフィックス　coldwater graphiix　S: シブヤパブリッシング＆セラーズ　SHIBUYA PUBLISHING & BOOKSELLERS

ショップカード　Shop Card

ブックディレクション / 出版 / ディストリビューション / イベント企画
Book Direction / Publishing / Distribution / Event Planning

本というメディアを通して新しいものを生み出していくBACHは、幅 允孝を中心として、ブックディレクション、出版、ディストリビューション、イベント企画など幅広い分野で活動している。名刺・封筒・会社設立案内・移転案内等の自社ツールは、スープ・デザインが制作。名刺にはケナフを使用し、会社設立案内には、BACHのコンセプトが印刷されたポスターを同封、移転案内にはフリップブックを制作するなど、本という媒体と紙に対するこだわりを感じるツールとなっている。

BACH, which produces new work through the books, is led by Yoshitaka Haba and active in a wide range of fields such as book direction, publishing, distribution and event management. The company's business tools including the business card, envelopes, the company profile and the change of premises notice were produced by Soup Design. Kenaf was used for the business cards, a poster printed with the BACH concepts was enclosed with the company profile, and the change of premises notice was produced as a flipbook, to create a set of business tools that demonstrates a particular approach to the medium of books and paper.

Japan　CD: 幅 允孝 Yoshitaka Haba　AD: 尾原史和 Fumikazu Ohara　DF: スープ・デザイン SOUP DESIGN　S: バッハ BACH

設立案内 Establishment Invitation

移転案内 Moving Announcement

We moved.
And we've got to make new book shelves!
引越しました。どんどん新しい本棚をつくらなくっちゃ!

love printed matter. BACH

FRAME Publisher

出版社
Publisher

FRAME PublisherとはFrame Magazine含むインテリア関係の雑誌や本を発行する出版社。最新のインテリア情報を発信するFrame Magazineのロゴには11種類の色とパターンを使って、流動的で流行に敏感な社のアイデンティティーを表現した。

Frame Publisher is the publisher of Frame magazine and other trade books on interior design. The logo is designed to represent Frame's identity as a publishing house in "flux", writing about cutting edge interior design. 11 different patterns in 11 different colors are used to support the "in flux" idea of Frame's activities.

USA   CD, AD, DF, S: COMA Amsterdam / New York

Marcel Hermans
Art Director

COMA   T +31 (0)20 6928 277
Saxenburgerstraat 21-1   F +31 (0)20 6923 659
1054 KN Amsterdam   coma@aya.yale.edu
The Netherlands   www.comalive.com

Cornelia Blatter
Art Director

COMA   T +1 718 3499 783
121 Dobbin Street #4R   F +1 718 3499 783
Brooklyn, NY 11222   coma@aya.yale.edu
USA   www.comalive.com

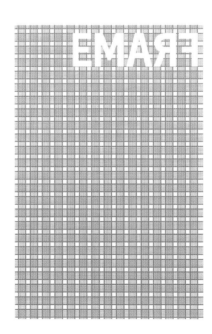

Frame Publishers   T +31 (0)20 4233 717   Chamber of Commerce
Lijnbaansgracht 87   F +31 (0)20 4280 653   Amsterdam 34153782
1015 GZ Amsterdam   info@framemag.com   VAT NL 809616981B01
The Netherlands   www.framemag.com   ING Bank 65841896

'Frame for me – from the first issue on – was a very refreshing publication within this field, and I still feel the same about it. Courageous, with different perspectives or attitudes than others. Bravo! Go on like that!'
Ingo Maurer

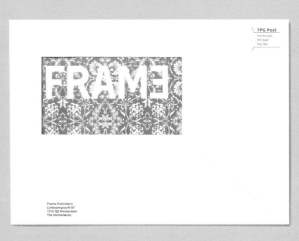

what is *frame*?

Frame magazine shows you what's happening and where to find it.

The hottest spaces, the coolest products, spiced up with slices of art and architecture: that's the essence of *Frame* magazine. We gather the most radical and fashionable work from around the globe and package it to perfection in six hefty issues a year. Loaded with nothing but the best in contemporary design, Frame is an inspiring and indispensable reference for professionals in interior design and other creative pursuits.
Frame magazine should be the anchor in your media plan. No other design magazine reaches a worldwide readership of nearly 100,000 top-level interior design professionals.

editorial formula
Each issue of *Frame* is built on the following sections.
• Details: Concise portraits of newly completed interiors worldwide, from Tokyo hair salons to the latest bars in London.
• Portrait: Every issue features an in-depth story of an up-and-coming interior designer or architect.
• Features: Articles on recently created hot spots, innovative design and even a bit of art.
• Products: Frame brings you the latest products – from furniture and lighting designs to display systems and fabrics – in its products section. Visitors to our website can request free info about these products.

awards
From the outset, Frame has put a great deal of effort into making the magazine look different than others. To date, collaboration with art directors Roelof Mulder and COMA has resulted in two awards.
• The Art Directors Club (ADC) 83nd Annual Awards: 2003 Merit Award.
• The Society of Publication Designers (SPD): 2004 Silver Medal for Magazine of the Year.

会社案内 Company Brochure

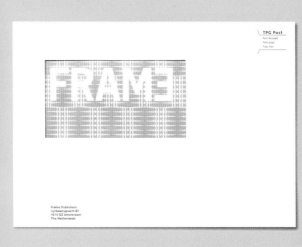

135

ロースター　Roaster Co. Ltd.

フリーペーパーやカタログ制作を中心とする、広告及び雑誌制作会社。社名は「豆の煎り方によって美味しくなるコーヒーがあるように、本とウェブの編集も素材の調理の仕方で全く違うものになる」という意味を込めてつけられた。自社ツールの作成は、博報堂のアートディレクター・長嶋りかこが担当。素材を大切にする、こだわりあるコーヒーショップを思わせる素朴なロゴと、シンプルなマグカップのシンボルマークが見事に調和し、幅広く使用することが可能となっている。(http://roaster.co.jp)

A magazine production company dealing mainly in free papers and catalogue production. The company name contains the idea of "just as coffee relies for its flavor on the way the beans are roasted, books turn out completely differently depending on the way they are edited." Art director, Rikako Nagashima of Hakuhodo Co. Ltd. was responsible for the creation of the company's business tools. The simple logo, which makes us think of a coffee shop and is particular about materials, and the simple emblem of the coffee mug harmonize wonderfully and can be applied to a number of situations.

Japan　AD, D, S: 長嶋りかこ Rikako Nagashima　D: 水溜友絵 Tomoe Mizutamari　Printing: 鈴木 登（日光プロセス）Noboru Suzuki (Nikko Process Co., Ltd.)　DF: シロップ Syrup inc.

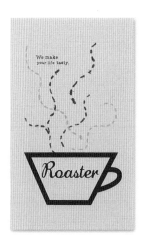

We make
your life tasty.

Roaster

Roaster

Roaster

We make
your life tasty.

ポスター Poster

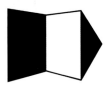

ドリルデザイン　DRILL DESIGN

林 裕輔と安西葉子により2000年に設立されたデザインスタジオ。プロダクトデザインを中心に、グラフィックデザイン、パッケージデザイン、空間演出までトータルなデザインワークを行っている。自社ツールはCOILのアートディレクター・田中義久が担当。ステーショナリーにもプロダクト感を出したいという想いが、各ツールのアイデアソースとなっている。名刺は左端の一点を糊付けし、ブロック状にして立体感を出し、封筒は折り方によって色の組み合わせを変えられる仕様に。ロゴは、ふせんを折ってできたDの形をグラフィックにおとし込んだ。

A design studio established in 2000 by Yusuke Hayashi and Yoko Yasunishi offering a complete range of design services that includes graphic design, packaging design and space creation, with a focus on product design. The idea for each of the tools was to present the company's stationery as if it were a form of product. The business cards are glued along the left edge to form a three-dimensional block and the envelopes come in different combination of colors depending on the way they are folded. The logo, the shape of the letter D produced by folding the label, adds a graphic element.

Japan　AD, D: 田中義久　Yoshihisa Tanaka　DF, S: コイル　COIL inc.

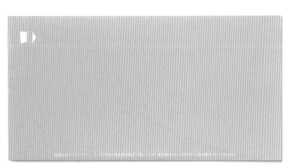

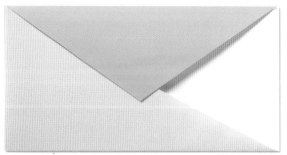

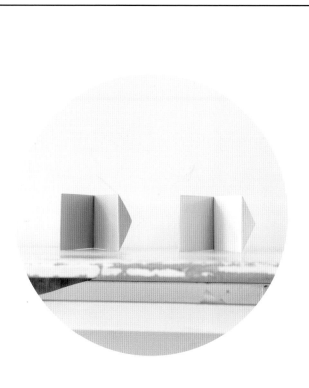

ポスター (箔押し加工に沿って折っていくと、DRILL DESIGNのロゴができあがる仕組みとなっている。)
Poster (Designed so that the DRILL DESIGN logo appears when folded along the foil.)

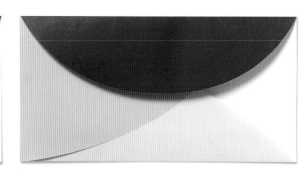

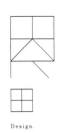

ONDA Design.

ショップの空間デザインなどを手がけるインテリアデザイン事務所。ロゴや自社ツールは、6Dのアートディレクター・木住野彰悟が制作。シャープで幅のあるデザインを感じさせるべく、社名である「恩田デザイン」の「恩田」の文字をできる限り少ない情報でデザインし、色もスミ1色に設定した。ステーショナリーもロゴと同様シンプルに。ポスターや年賀状はフリーハンドを感じさせる、動きのあるデザインとし、他ツールとのギャップを狙った。

An interior design office dealing in retail space design. Art director Shogo Kishino of 6D produced the logo and the company's business tools. To create an image of sharp, versatile design, the "Onda" in the company name Onda Design has been produced with a minimum of information in black. The stationery has the same simplicity as the logo. The posters and New Year cards have a design with a freehand look, their aim being to fill the gaps of other business tools.

Japan　AD, D: 木住野彰悟 Shogo Kishino　DF, S: ロクディ 6D

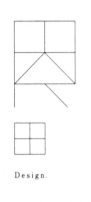

年賀状 New Year Card

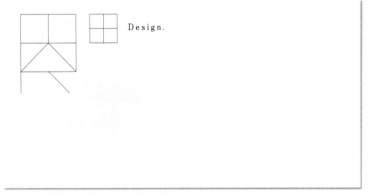

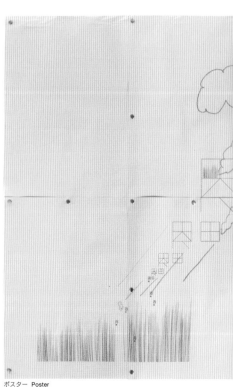

ポスター Poster

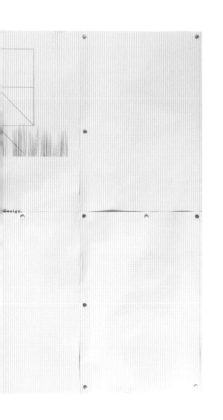

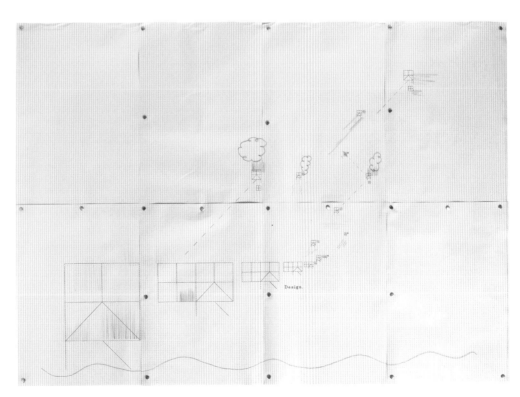

Cukrowicz Nachbaur Architekten

Cukrowicz Nachbaur Architektenはオーストリアに所在する建築事務所。ロゴは創立者の頭文字Cukrowiczの「C」とNachbaurの「N」を用いてデザインされている。オフィスステーショナリーはシンプルな白黒で統一され、ビジネスカードには特殊な紙を使用し、文字は箔押しされている。

Cukrowicz Nachbaur Architekten is an architecture bureau located in Austria. Logo is designed with first letters of the founder's name "Cukrowicz" and "Nachbaur". Office stationeries are unified in simple black and white coloring. Business card is made with special paper with hot foil stamping technique.

Austria   AD, D: Sigi Ramoser   D: Silvia Keckeis   DF, S: SÄGENVIER

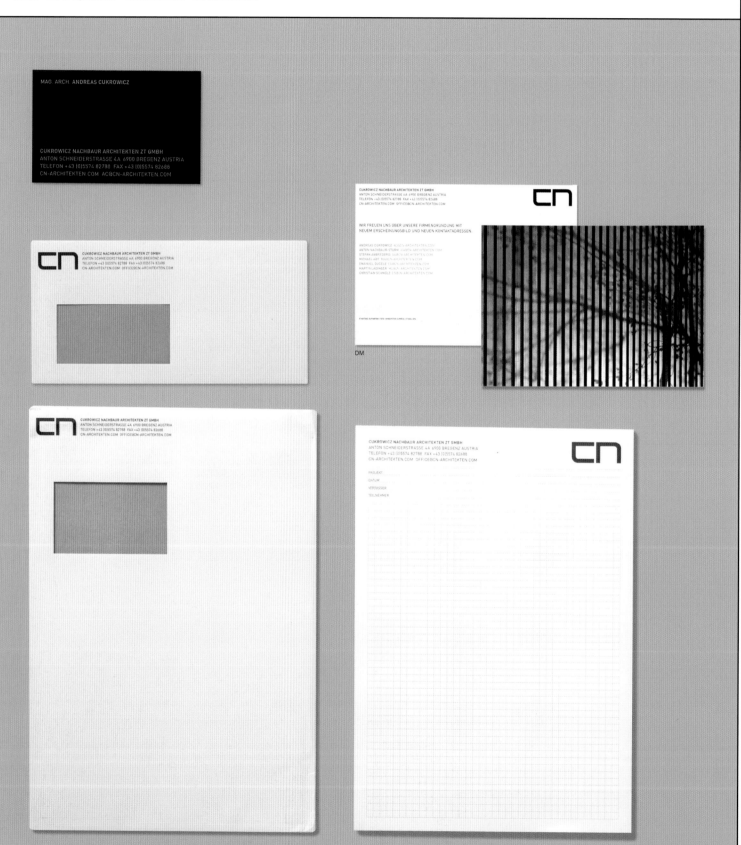

DM

ArkOpen Ltd.

建築デザイン、リノベーションや都市開発のリサーチやプランニングを手がけるArk Open Ltd.は、居住者の意見や希望を積極的に取り入れたオープンな姿勢で建築物を手がけるフィンランド屈指の建築事務所。様々な素材と紙を用い、素材に応じてシルクスクリーンもしくはオフセット印刷で制作されたオフィスステーショナリーには、多種多様の建築物を造る彼らのワークスタイルが反映されている。

ArkOpen Ltd. is an architecture bureau whose field of work includes architecture design, town planning, renovation, development and research. ArkOpen is the leading bureau in Finland when it comes to open architecture where inhabitants themselves can choose e.g. the plan and the materials of their apartment. For the office stationeries, a selection of various papers and materials is used to reflect this freedom of choise. Silkscreen and offset were used depending on the paper and material.

Finland   AD, D: Antti Raudaskoski   D: Paco Aguayo   DF, S: Hahmo Design Ltd.

ファイル File

カード Card

ジオグラフ　GEOGRAPH

設計デザイン / プロダクトデザイン / グラフィックデザイン
Architect / Product Design / Graphic Design

高木隆亘と加藤匡毅を中心として設立されたジオグラフは、建築やインテリアをはじめとする設計デザイン、プロダクトデザイン、グラフィックデザインなど幅広い分野で活躍している。名刺はできる限りシンプルに、長く残るデザインを目指し、活版印刷の嘉瑞工房に依頼した。マスキングテープは、第2の名刺としてインフォメーションが印刷されており、封筒を閉じるときはもちろん、事務所入口のサインなど幅広く活用できる仕組みとなっている。

Geograph established by Takanobu Takagi and Masaki Kato is active in a wide range of fields including architectural and interior design, product design, and graphic design. The business cards have been kept as simple as possible, and with the aim of being able to use the design for a long time, Kazui Press was commissioned to do the letterpress printing. The Geograph logo has been printed on masking tape used for sealing the envelopes, as well as in the company's signage at the entrance to its offices.

Japan　　D, DF, S: ジオグラフ　GEOGRAPH

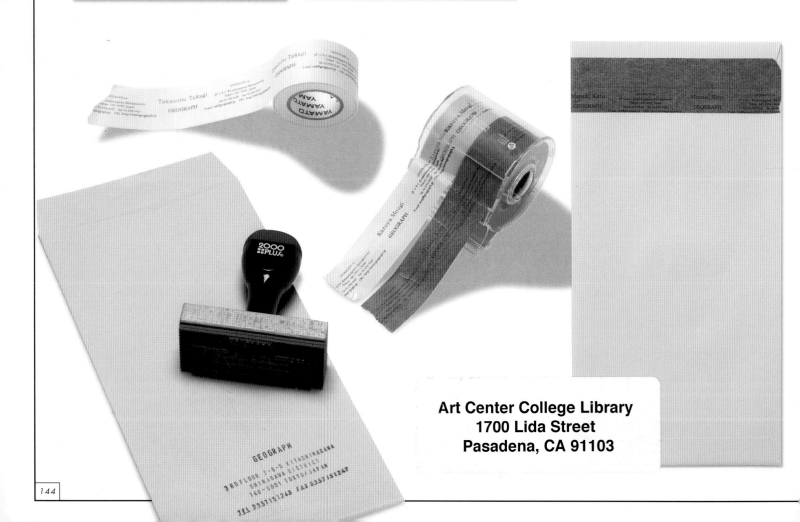

亜意舎建築設計諮詢有限公司　A-I-SHA ARCHITECTS

建築デザイン
Architect

上海を拠点に活動中の建築家・藤岡 務が2005年に設立した建築設計事務所。自社ツール（名刺・封筒・レターヘッド・DM）の作成は、「氏デザイン」が担当。ロゴデザインは、社名の「亜」の文字をモチーフに、建築の鉄骨や中国の古典家具をイメージした形態となっている。自社ツールには色を使用せず、すべてモノクロームで展開。社名やURLにオリジナルのフォントを使って統一感を出している。

An architectural design office established by architect, Tsutomu Fujioka who is currently working out of Shanghai. ujidesign was responsible for the production of the company's business tools (business cards, envelopes, letterhead, DM). The logo is designed around the steel frame of a building with a motif of the first character of the company name. The business tools are in various shades of a single color and an original font has been used for the company name and the URL to achieve a sense of consistency.

China　AD, DF, S: 氏デザイン　ujidesign

上海創青建築工程設計有限公司　Sosei Consaltant

建築外装設計コンサルタント
Facade Design Consultant

カーテンウォール（ビルなどの高層建築物の外壁などに用いられる非耐力壁）を専門とする設計コンサルタント会社。自社ツール（名刺・封筒）の作成は、「氏デザイン」が担当。ユニークで幅広い展開を見せる設計コンサルタントらしい柔軟な発想で作られたツールは、光を反射するガラスカーテンウォールをイメージしたライトグレーのチェックを基調とし、社名の青ではなくあえて赤を用いてシンプルかつエレガントな仕上がりとなっている。

An architectural design office specializing in the design of curtain walls (non-load bearing walls used for the outer walls of high-rise structures). ujidesign was responsible for the production of the company's business tools (business cards, envelopes). The business tools created from the versatile ideas that one would expect to see from a design office that demonstrates a unique and diverse range of design is based on a light grey check to resemble a curtain wall, producing a simple yet impressive result.

創青

Japan　AD, DF, S: 氏デザイン　ujidesign

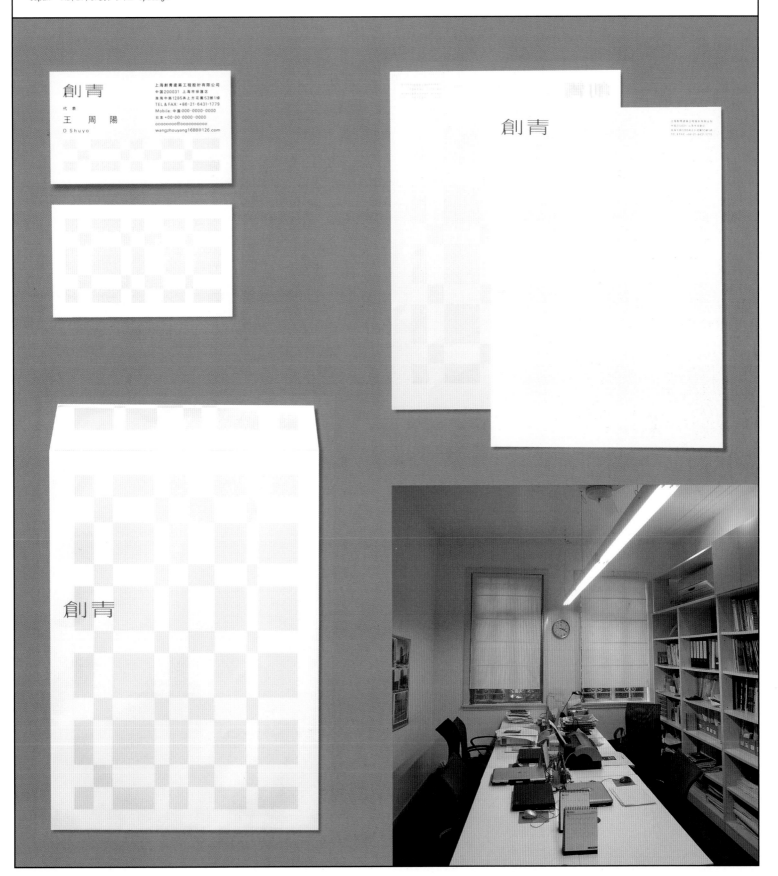

キラメキ　kirameki inc.

映像制作会社
Audiovisual Production Company

映像プロデューサー・石井義樹が率いる映像制作会社。TVCMやミュージックビデオなど、映像・グラフィックの企画制作を手掛けている。社員のほとんどがバイリンガルなので、海外のクリエイターや監督を起用する機会が多い。ロゴには社名の「キラメキ」をそのままかたどったデザインを採用。そのロゴを基に展開した自社ツールは名刺、封筒、レターヘッド、紙袋、グリーティングカード、会社案内など多数。封筒類は内側にロゴの柄を印刷し、中が透けて見えるデザインになっている。

An audiovisual production company led by audiovisual producer, Yoshiki Ishii. The company deals in audiovisual and graphic design planning and production including television commercials and music videos with creators and directors hired from overseas, as well as serving as a liaison between overseas creators on the one hand and Japanese agencies and clients on the other. The design of the logo contains the words "Kirameki" and based on the logo, a large number of business tools have been produced for the company. A pattern made from the logo has been printed on the inside of the envelopes, having the effect of making the inside appear transparent.

Japan　　CD, AD: 後 智仁 Tomohito Ushiro　　D: 柳川敬介 Keisuke Yanagawa　　P: 高橋秀行 Hideyuki Takahashi　　DF: sude, ltd.　　S: キラメキ kirameki inc.

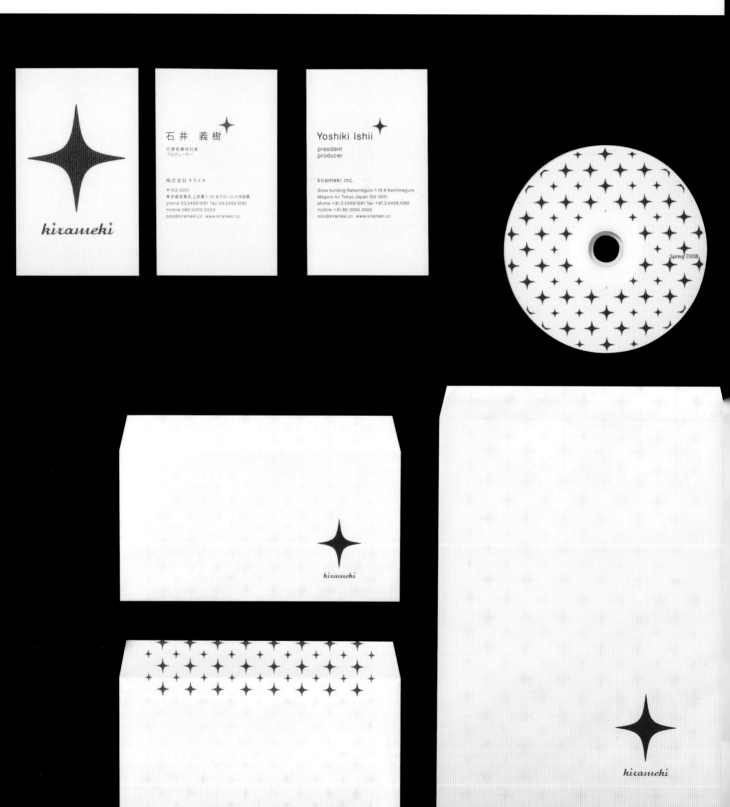

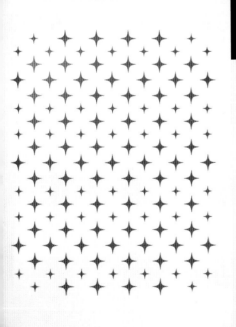

hirameki

ファイル File

A-ASTERISK

上海を拠点に活動中の建築家・中村誠宏が2005年に設立した建築設計事務所。自社ツール（名刺・封筒・レターヘッド・会社案内）の作成は、「氏デザイン」が担当。ロゴデザインは、社名の「A」の文字をデザイン化したもの。自社ツールには色を使用せず、すべてモノクロームで展開し、社名やURLにオリジナルのフォントを使って統一感を出している。また、日本人建築家ということを意識し、名刺には浮世絵を使用している。

An architectural design office established in 2005 by architect, Nobuhiro Nakamura who is currently working from a base in Shanghai. ujidesign was responsible for the production of the company's business tools (business card, envelopes, letterhead, company profile). The letter A of the company's name has been made a feature of the logo design. The business tools are in various shades of a single color and an original font has been used for the company name and the URL to achieve a sense of consistency. Ukiyo-e prints have been used on the business cards so that people are aware that the architect is Japanese.

China   AD, DF, S: 氏デザイン ujidesign

nendo

佐藤オオキを中心に2002年に設立されたデザインオフィス。建築からインテリア、家具、プロダクト、CIデザインまで幅広い活動を行っている。事務所名は、自由にこねられる粘土を柔軟な発想の象徴としてとらえ、ジャンルを超えてボーダーレスに活動していく、という意味を込めた。名刺、封筒、ファイルなどの自社ツールには、粘土のような質感のハンマートーンGAを使用。ワークスペースは、壁のない見通しのよいスペースを意識し、楕円形の仕切りを各スペースに配置した。

A design office established in 2002 and headed up by Oki Sato, involved in a wide range of activity from architecture to interior, furniture, product and CI design. The Japanese word "nendo" means "clay," a malleable substance to symbolize flexible thinking and contains the idea of working in a way that transcends genres. Hammertone GA paper that resembles paper clay has been used in the company's business tools (business cards, envelopes and files). The workspace has been arranged for openness and visibility with an oval-shaped threshold placed in front of each individual work area.

Japan   AD, D, S: nendo   P: 阿野太一 Daichi Ano

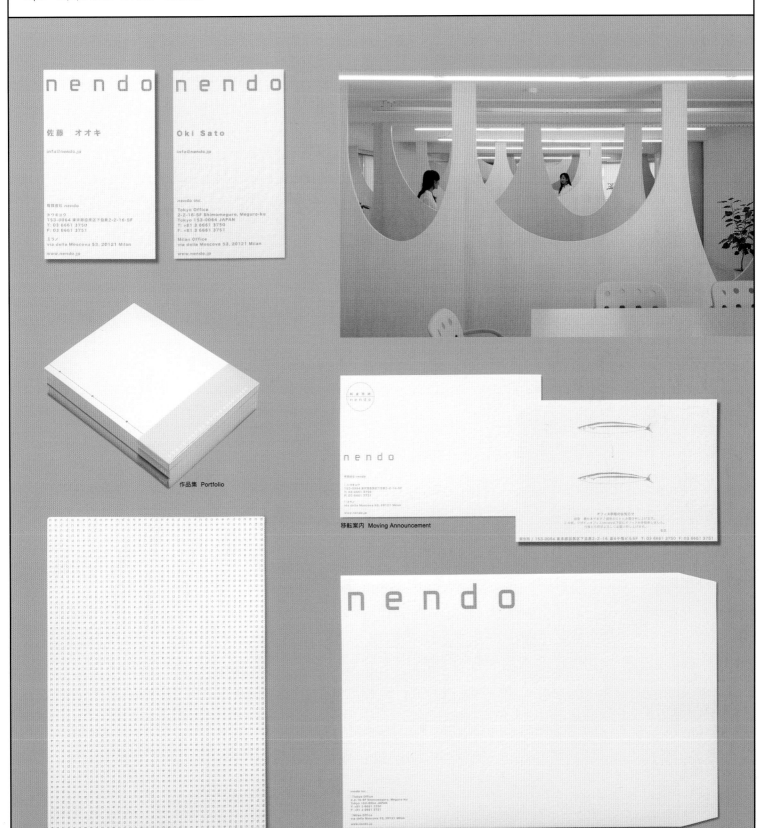

作品集 Portfolio

移転案内 Moving Announcement

ファイル File

REC SOUNDDESIGN

REC SOUNDDESIGNはアムステルダムに所在するサウンドデザインスタジオ。ロゴデザインにはオーディオやビデオテープに見られるステッカーの形を用いている。また便箋のステッカーは、郵便物に貼るなど自由に使える。名刺は社員3名の名前が載った1種類で、渡すときに他2名の名前を剥がして使うようになっている。

REC SOUNDDESIGN is a sound design studio based in Amsterdam. Logo design derives from audio and videotape stickers. Stickers on the stationeries can be used on couriers to personalize message. The company has only one business card containing the three names of the employees. Every employee can remove the names of his colleagues in order to make it his own business card.

Netherlands   D: Peter Van Den Hoogen / Erica Terpstra   DF, S: COUP

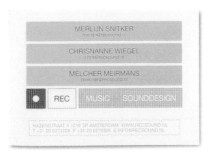

ステッカー Sticker

ステッカー Sticker

カード Card

Thurm & Dinges

Thurm & Dingesはドイツに所在する建築事務所。信頼性と堅実性を表現するために、ロゴはDINの大文字を使用し、そして鈍くならないようにシアンを用いている。

Thurm & Dinges is an architect office based in Germany. Logo uses uppercase DIN to give a solid and reliable feel and Cyan to not to become dull.

Germany　D: Billy Kiossoglou / Frank Philippin　DF, S: Brighten the Corners

ステッカー
Sticker

ドアーズ doors

広告・映像の企画制作
Advertising & Audiovisual Production Company

2001年に小林俊明により設立された、広告、映像、デジタルコンテンツの企画制作会社。21世紀の始まりとともに設立されたため、新たな扉を開くという意味を込めて、「ドアーズ」と命名した。ロゴをはじめ、名刺・封筒など自社ツールのデザインはグラフィックデザイン事務所・デイリー・フレッシュによるもの。また、トランプやグラス、トートバッグなどのノベルティは、スタッフなどへの季節の挨拶として制作している。

A planning and production company for advertising, audio-visual and digital content, established in 2001 by Toshiaki Kobayashi. As it was established at the start of the 21st century, the company was named Doors to symbolize the opening of a new door. The company's business tools including the logo, the business cards and envelopes were produced by the graphic design office, Daily Fresh. A range of novelties that includes playing cards, drinking glasses and tote bags is produced and sent to the staffs as season's greetings.

Japan   AD, D: 秋山具義 Gugi Akiyama   DF: デイリー・フレッシュ Dairy Fresh   S: ドアーズ doors

グラス Glass

トランプ
Playing Cards

ステッカー Sticker

封筒 Envelope

キリフダ　KIRIFUDA Inc.

ウェブ制作
Web Design

キリフダは、インターネットメディアの企画および運営を行うウェブ総合コンサルティング会社。「キリフダ」という社名は、特別な場面で特別な力を発揮する、頼れる存在になるという意味を込めて、電通テックのコピーライターである菊池雄也が命名した。名刺のデザインは、同じく電通テックの隈部 浩が担当。コシの強い紙を使い、両面PP加工にすることでトランプ感を演出。トランプと同数の53種類のマークとメッセージが印刷された名刺は、手に取る者に喜びと驚きをプレゼントする。

Kirifuda Inc. is a general Web consulting company offering Internet media planning and management services. The company was named Kirifuda by Kikuchi Yuya, formerly a copywriter for Dentsu Tec Inc. and means a reliable presence that demonstrates special capability in special situations. Hiroshi Kumabe, also of Dentsu Tec, was responsible for the design of the business cards. Both sides of a sheet of sturdy card underwent a polypropylene lamination to produce a playing card effect. The business cards printed with 53 kinds of marks and messages, the same as in a pack of playing cards, produce happiness and surprise in the people to whom they are given.

Japan　　AD: 隈部 浩 Hiroshi Kumabe　　CW: 菊池雄也 Yuya Kikuchi　　DF, S: 電通テック DENTSU TEC INC.

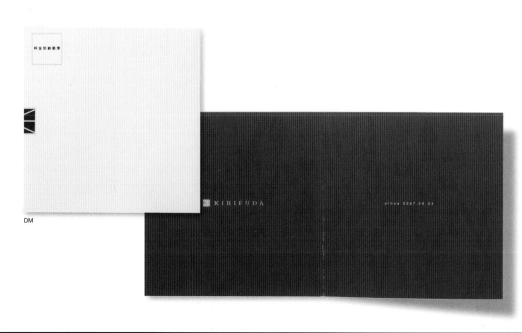

DM

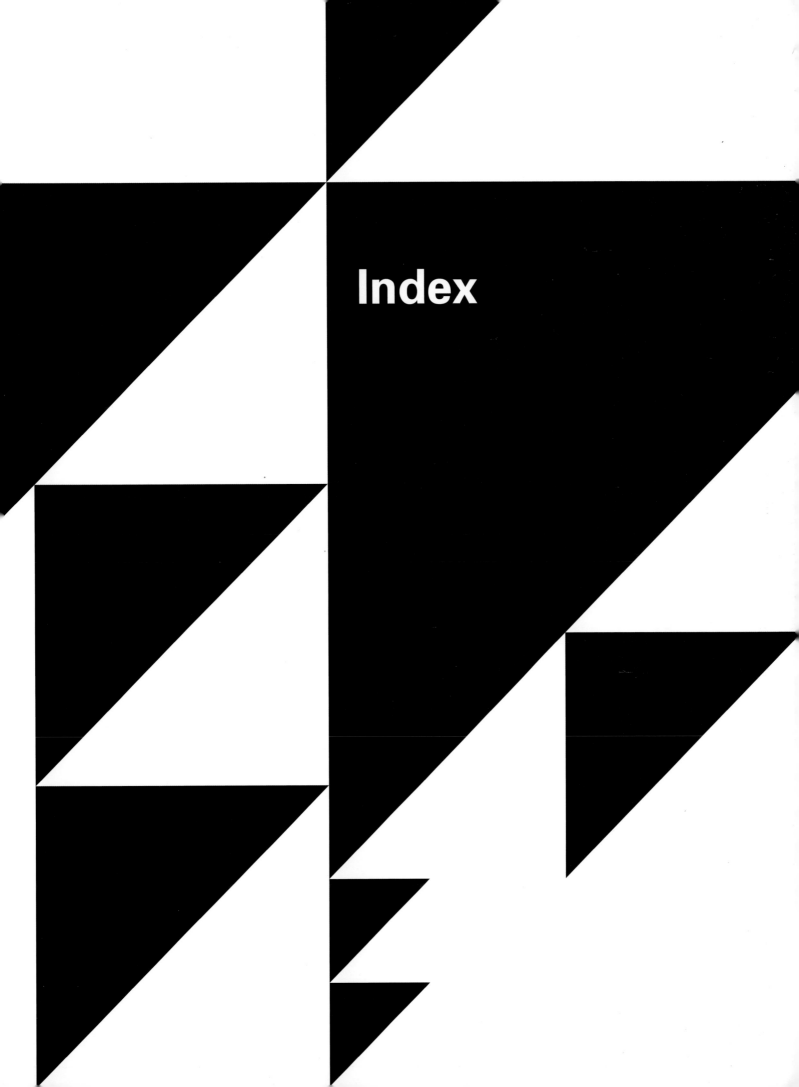

Index

Index

クリエイターの自社ツール＆ワークスペース
Creators' Self-Promotion: In-House Graphics

JACKET DESIGN
尾原史和（スープ・デザイン）
Fumikazu Ohara (SOUP DESIGN inc.)

ART DIRECTOR
柴 亜季子
Akiko Shiba

DESIGNER
高松セリアサユリ
Célia Sayuri Takamatsu

COORDINATOR & WRITER
田端宏章 Hiroaki Tabata
金城佳代子 Kayoko Kinjo
白倉三紀子 Mikiko Shirakura

TRANSLATOR
パメラ・ミキ Pamela Miki

PHOTOGRAPHER
藤本邦治 Kuniharu Fujimoto
藤牧徹也 Tetsuya Fujimaki
（Offices p. 011, 033, 063, 072, 083, 087, 101,
115, 123, 127, 129, 133, 137, 141, 145, 155）

EDITOR
宮崎亜美 Ami Miyazaki

PUBLISHER
三芳伸吾 Shingo Miyoshi

2008年9月9日 初版第1刷発行

PIE BOOKS
2-32-4, Minami-Otsuka,
Toshima-ku, Tokyo 170-0005 Japan

Tel: ＋81-3-5395-4811
Fax: ＋81-3-5395-4812
e-mail: editor@piebooks.com
　　　　sales@piebooks.com
http://www.piebooks.com

発行所 ピエ・ブックス
〒170-0005 東京都豊島区南大塚2-32-4
編集 Tel: 03-5395-4820
　　　Fax: 03-5395-4821
　　　e-mail: editor@piebooks.com

営業 Tel: 03-5395-4811
　　　Fax: 03-5395-4812
　　　e-mail: sales@piebooks.com
http://www.piebooks.com

印刷・製本 図書印刷株式会社